Guidelines

Questions and Answers about the laws of BISHUL

Guidelines

Questions and Answers
about the laws of
BISHUL

Rabbi Elozor Barclay
Rabbi Yitzchok Jaeger

MENUCHA
PUBLISHERS

A Menucha Press Book

First published 2015
Copyright © 2015 by E. Barclay & Y. Jaeger
ISBN 978-1-61465-480-3

Please address any questions or comments
regarding the GUIDELINES books to the authors:
E. Barclay (02) 583 0914
Y. Jaeger (02) 583 4889
email: 5834889@gmail.com

VOLUMES IN THE GUIDELINES SERIES:

TEFILLAH VOLUME ONE	**BRACHOS VOLUME ONE**
TEFILLAH VOLUME TWO	**BRACHOS VOLUME TWO**
MAJOR EVENTS OF LIFE	**HONORING PARENTS**
FAMILY PURITY	**THE THREE WEEKS**
SHEMITTAH	**YOMIM NORAIM**
YOM TOV	**CHANUKAH**
PESACH	**SUCCOS**
BORER	**PURIM**
BISHUL	**YICHUD**

KIDDUSH AND HAVDALAH
THE GUIDELINES HAGGADAH
SEFIRAS HA'OMER & SHAVUOS
CANDLE LIGHTING & SEPARATING CHALLAH

Published by:
Menucha Publishers Inc.
250 44th street Suite #B2
Brooklyn N.Y. 11232
Tel/Fax: 718-232-0856
1-855-Menucha
sales@menuchapublishers.com
www.menuchapublishers.com

(Translation of Hebrew Original)

Rabbi CHAIM P. SCHEINBERG
Rosh Hayeshiva "TORAH ORE"
and Morah Hora'ah of Kiryat Mattersdorf

בס"ד, חודש שבט, תשס"ג

מכתב ברכה

I was pleased to see **"Guidelines"**, an impressive six volume work which encompasses the *halachos* of the *Moadim* and other relevant topics, written by Rabbi Elozor Barclay, *shlita* and Rabbi Yitzchok Jaeger, *shlita*. These books have been praised highly by numerous *Gedolei HaRabbonim* and have been received warmly by the English speaking Torah community.

As a matter of policy, I do not endorse *halachic* rulings in any published *sefer*. However, since so many *Gedolei Torah* have already agreed to what is written and offered their approbation to **"Guidelines"**, I join them and offer my heartfelt blessing that *Hashem* should guide and assist the authors in producing more successful *halachic* works, which glorify and strengthen the Torah.

Signed in the honor of the Torah,

Rabbi Chaim Pinchas Scheinberg

2 Panim Meirot St., Jerusalem, P.O.B. 6979, Tel. (02) 537-1513, Israel

*Letter of Approbation received from
Rabbi Nachman Bulman zt"l for Guidelines to Succos*

Rabbi Nachman Bulman
Yeshivat Ohr Somayach
Beit Knesset Nachliel

רב נחמן בולמן
מנהל רוחני ישיבת אור שמח
רב ק"ק נחליאל נוה יעקב מזרח

בע"ה

יום ו', י"ח תמוז, תשס"ב פה עיה"ק ת"ו

Friday, eighteenth of Tammuz, 5762, the holy city of
Yerushalayim.

I was delighted to see the fifth volume of the
Guidelines series. The questions and answers in
Guidelines provide a clear and easily understood
format and clarify relevant halachic issues.

It is clear from the quality of this work that Rabbi
Elozor Barclay and Rabbi Yitzchok Jaeger have
invested great amounts of time and effort in their
thorough investigation of these dinim. Every
answer has been written carefully and thoughtfully,
considering both the classic and the most up-to-
date halachic authorities. The accurate Hebrew
references will certainly be an invaluable aid for
any reader who wishes to investigate further.

I highly recommend this book to any person who is
truly searching to know the correct conduct.

Signed with admiration,

נחמן בולמן

מנהל רוחני ישיבת אור שמח
רב ק"ק נחליאל נוה יעקב מזרח ביום הנ"ל
ועיני נשואות לשמים להסכמת שוכן במרומים

משה הלברשטאם

חבר הבד"ץ העדה החרדית

ראש ישיבת "דברי חיים" טשאקאווע

מח"ס שו"ת "דברי משה"

פעיה"ק ירושלים תובב"א

רח' יואל 8 טל. 5370514

בס"ד

ערב ט"ו בשבט לסדר "והיה ביום השישי" תשס"ג לפ"ק

מאד שמחתי ונהנתי כשהובאו לפני ליקוטים נפלאים לעת עתה
על הלכות פורים, פסח, ימים נוראים, סוכה וחנוכה ואי"ה עוד
יד נטוי' להשלים המלאכה, שחיברו האברכים החשובים חו"ב
מוהר"ר אלעזר ברקלי שליט"א ומוהר"ר יצחק ייגר שליט"א
אוצר בלום מה שאספו וליקטו הלכות רבות ונחוצות מהשו"ע
ונושאי כליו מספרי הפוסקים ראשונים ואחרונים מסודר
בתבונה והשכל בטטו"ד לתועלת וזיכוי הרבים.

ונוכחתי לראות כי הלכו מישרים לאסוקי שמעתתא אליבא
דהלכתא והיטב אשר עשו שציינו מקור לכל הלכה והלכה
למען אשר כבר הזהירו גאוני קדמאי שלא לפסוק הלכה
למעשה מספרי הקיצורים.

ואמינא לפעלא טבא יישר כוחם וחילם לאורייתא והנני נותן
להם בזה ברכת מור"ר הגה"צ שליט"א שיזכו להמשיך לעלות
במעלות התורה להו"ל עוד חיבורים יקרים ולזכות את הרבים
מתוך נחת ושפע ברכות והצלחה, אכי"ר.

ובעה"ח בפקודת הקודש

יהונתן וינר

מו"ץ בבית הוראה

שע"י מרן הגה"צ שליט"א

נ.ב. בספר על הלכות חנוכה שאלה 15, בגדר איסור מלאכה לנשים
בחנוכה עיין בן איש חי פרשת וישב סי' כז, וט"ז ס' תרע סק"ב דמשמע
דומיא דר"ח, וכן שמעתי מכרכא דכולי ביה מרא דכולא תלמודא (לשון
מוהר"ר הגה"צ בשו"ת דברי משה ס' יד) ממוה"ר חיים קנייבסקי שליט"א.

Rabbi E. Falk

146 Whitehall Road
Gateshead NE8 1TP
England

פסח אליהו פאלק

דומ״ץ בקהי״ק גייטסהעד יצ״ו
מחה״ס שו״ת מחזה אליהו
יזכור ושמור׳ על הלכות שבת
יעוז והדר לבושה׳ על הל׳ צניעות דלבוש

בס״ד

20 Kisleiv 5765 - Gateshead UK

Once again a great service has been rendered to the Jewish English-speaking public by the great "partners in *zikuy harabim*" - Rabbi Elozor Barclay *shlita* and Rabbi Yitzchok Jaeger *shlita*. They have prepared a sefer on the laws of *tefilla* - thereby giving the person who is praying easy access to the numerous intricate laws that could apply to him at any point during his prayers. With this production they have earned themselves an enormous merit, for *tefilla* is a duty that stands towering above everything else (See *Gemara Brachos* 32b), and to ensure the correct execution of such a duty by a multitude of people, is an immeasurable merit.

As with their other works in the **"Guidelines"** series, this *sefer* is concise, accurate, and well structured. The authors have performed a great service, presenting these vital and complex laws in a clear and straightforward questions and answers format. This style arouses the interest and opens the mind, enabling the reader to fully integrate the information. As clarity of material assists the memory, the person who learns the relevant *halachos* in this manner is likely to remember them and know exactly how to react when a given situation arises.

Unfortunately, my busy schedule does not allow me to thoroughly review every *halacha*, and therefore I cannot accept personal responsibility for the rulings given. However, the authors have themselves invested vast amounts of time and effort researching the sources and clarifying the laws. Apart from this, they have had access to the excellent *seforim* that have been published on the laws of *tefilla* over the last two decades. I am therefore confident that the *halachos* have been correctly presented and I add my approval to its printing for the benefit of the public.

May *Hashem Yisborach* bless the authors with great success in the publication of this work, and other works that they will produce *b'ezer Hashem* in the future. I pray that this *sefer* will be warmly accepted and will lead to increased appreciation and greater dedication to the great gift *Hashem Yisborach* has given us - the means to approach Him thrice daily and present our needs to Him through the medium of *tefilla*.

With Torah blessings,

Rabbi Pesach Eliyahu Falk

הרב רפאל צבי ובר

רב דקהילת קמניץ

ונוה יעקב מזרח, ירושלים

ז׳ כסלו תשס״ד

בס״ד

מכתב ברכה

שמחתי לראות ששני תלמידי חכמים יקרים הרב אלעזר ברקלי שליט״א והרב יצחק ייגר שליט״א חיברו ספר פסקי הלכות בשפה האנגלית.

וכבר זכו לחבר פסקי הלכות על המועדים שהתפרסמו הרבה, וזיכו את הרבים. ויש תועלת רבה בצורת הכתיבה בלשון שאלות ותשובות ועי״ז מתבררת ההלכה היטב.

ואע״פ שאיני מבין שפה האנגלית, אבל אני מכירם ויודעם בהשתדלות לאסוקי שמעתתא אליבא דהלכתא, ונשאו ונתנו אתי בהרבה נושאים, והנני מברכם שיקבלו דבריהם בביהמ״ד.

בברכת התורה,

צבי ובר

RABBI ZEV LEFF
Rabbi of Moshav Matisyahu
Rosh Hayeshiva Yeshiva Gedola Matisyahu

בס"ד

תמוז תשס"ז

It is with great pleasure that I have received the latest addition to the series of Halachic Guides produced by Rabbi Elozor Barclay שליט"א and Rabbi Yitzchok Jaeger שליט"א - **Guidelines** to Shemittah.

This is an impressive work which will serve as an invaluable aid to those who seek to be guided through the shemittah year.

As in the previous volumes the laws are lucidly and concisely presented in a manner that will serve as a guide and source for the beginner and a source of review for the advanced student. I highly recommend this work as all the other volumes of this series.

May Hashem grant the authors long life and health and ability to continue to merit Klal Yisroel with the promulgation of Torah and mitzvos.

With Torah blessings,

Rabbi Zev Leff

Table of Contents

Foreword

With praise and thanks to Hashem, we continue the Guidelines series on the laws of Shabbos with the present volume on the *melacha* of bishul. Alongside the *melacha* of borer, which has already been covered by Guidelines, bishul qualifies equally as a *melacha* whose laws are complex and yet extremely applicable.

The Chafetz Chaim zt"l, in his introduction to the *halachos* of Shabbos in the Mishna Brura, mentions bishul as a prime example of a *melacha* that people frequently transgress due to a lack of knowledge.

When one of the thirty-nine *melachos* has been transgressed, *Chazal* sometimes impose a penalty forbidding anyone to have benefit from such an act. The details depend on whether the error was deliberate or accidental, and whether it was forbidden by the Torah or by *Chazal* (see Chapter Thirteen). It is interesting to note that the example given by the Talmud and the Shulchan Aruch is the *melacha* of bishul. Perhaps this is an indication of how common mistakes are in this area, and that *Chazal* wanted to stress the importance of mastering this vital section of the laws of Shabbos.

Using the traditional Guidelines Question and Answer style, we have attempted to present the laws in a clear and systematic manner and have provided numerous examples that demonstrate the application of each concept.

Rarely will a written work be a perfect substitute for a one-to-one discussion with a rav. The answer to a query often depends upon various factors that only further questioning can clarify. Even though much thought and effort has been invested in the phrasing and wording used, it is possible that *halachos* may be misunderstood or misconstrued. Our primary intent is to guide the reader through these laws, hence the title Guidelines.

We would like to express our thanks to Rav Yaakov Montrose *shlita*, author of the Halachic World series, who with his keen perception and comprehensive mastery of the topics provided many valuable changes and additions throughout the entire book. Many thanks also to Reb Yerachmiel Goldberg and Reb Pinchas Goldstein for meticulously checking the text.

It is our hope that in the merit of fulfilling the laws of Shabbos punctiliously, we will be worthy to experience the peace, prosperity, and blessings that are promised to those who guard the Shabbos.

Elozor Barclay   Yitzchok Jaeger

Iyar 5775

Chapter One
General Principles

1. What is bishul?

Bishul is one of the thirty-nine *melachos* that are forbidden by the Torah to be done on Shabbos. Literally, the word bishul means cooking, but the *melacha* is defined as changing the quality of an item by heat. In this *sefer* we will explain how this applies to foods, although bishul can also apply to non-foods.

2. Are there any practical applications to non-foods?

Yes. It is forbidden to heat wax until it melts or to heat metal until it is red hot. Therefore:

- If there are drops of wax on a plate, one must not pour hot water onto the plate in order to melt the wax.
- If one wishes to place a blech over a gas flame (see Question 231), one must not use a piece of foil or thin metal that will become red hot.
- If one wishes to sterilize a needle for removing a splinter, he must not insert the point into a flame since it will become red hot. Instead, he may pour boiling water over it from an urn. **Note:** Removing a splinter is forbidden if this will cause bleeding unless one is in pain.

3.   Are all foods subject to bishul?

Yes, even foods that can be eaten raw must not be cooked on Shabbos. For example: apples, carrots, peppers. Similarly, liquids are subject to bishul even though they are already fit for drinking. E.g. water.

4.   What if cooking spoils the food?

It is still forbidden Rabbinically to cook such food. E.g. lettuce.

5.   Are all methods of cooking included?

Yes. Bishul includes: boiling, baking, roasting, frying, steaming, and any other method that effects a change to the food. Even indirect forms of cooking are forbidden.

6.   What is meant by an indirect form of cooking?

This refers to a situation in which the original source of heat is not present. For example, to place a raw food inside a hot oven that is switched off or inside a hot pot of soup that has just been taken off the fire. Although the original fire is not being used to cook the food, this form of cooking is still forbidden by the Torah.

7.   May one cook food in the heat of the sun?

Yes. The Torah does not forbid this type of bishul since it is not the standard way to cook food. For example, one may place an egg on a plate to fry in the rays of the sun or heat up cold raw food in this way. *Chazal* did not forbid this unusual type of bishul since it will not lead people to think that regular cooking through fire is also permitted. However, *Chazal* did forbid cooking indirectly through the sun since this could lead to cooking indirectly through fire.

8.   What is an example of indirect sun heat?

A simple example is cooking an egg in sand that became hot from the sun. Although it is permitted to cook an egg in direct sunlight, it is forbidden to cook it in the hot sand since this is indirect sun heat. A more important and practical example is the use of solar heating panels for hot water. In this system, the sun heats metal pipes which then heat water running through them. Opening the hot water faucet is forbidden since this allows cold water into the pipes, which will then be cooked through indirect sun heat. In addition, if there is hot water in the tank, the cold water that enters will cook immediately on contact with the hot water. See also Questions 64-66.

9.   May one partially cook food?

The Torah *melacha* of bishul is transgressed when a raw food undergoes a significant improvement even if it does not become fully cooked. The minimum degree of change occurs when the food becomes edible in an emergency. This is known as *ma'achal ben drusai* - literally the food of Ben Drusai. This person was an infamous highwayman who would eat his food only partially cooked.

10. At what point does food become *ma'achal ben drusai*?

Opinions differ whether this means one third or one half cooked. However, this dispute is usually academic since it is Rabbinically forbidden to start cooking any raw food on Shabbos even if it does not become *ma'achal ben drusai*.

11. What if one accidentally started cooking a raw food?

It must be removed from the fire immediately. If the food does not become *ma'achal ben drusai*, he has not done a Torah transgression but only a Rabbinic one.

12. May one warm up a raw food?

Yes, but only in a place where it is impossible for the food to become hot and start to cook. It is forbidden to put it even for a moment in a place where it can become hot since one might forget about it and allow it to start cooking. For example, one must not put raw frozen strawberries on an urn or radiator to defrost if they could become hot there.

13. What is meant by hot?

Chazal established a critical temperature at which the *melacha* of bishul can take place. This is called *yad soledes bo*, literally the degree of heat from which the hand withdraws. No food can cook below this temperature no matter how soft it is, and all foods can cook at this temperature no matter how tough they are.

Note: Throughout this *sefer*, we shall refer to *yad soledes bo* as 'hot' and less than *yad soledes bo* as 'warm'.

14. What is the temperature of *yad soledes bo*?

The exact temperature is unknown. Although most people today would not withdraw their hand from heat less than 50°C (122° F), one cannot rely on this since people vary greatly in their sensitivity. Therefore, a range of temperatures has been given within which *yad soledes bo* definitely falls. According to most opinions this is from 43°C to 71°C (110°F to 160°F). Due to the doubt, one must always use the figure that is more stringent. In most situations this means that 43°C (110°F) is considered hot and only below this is considered warm. Therefore, it is forbidden to place a raw food near a source of heat if it could eventually reach the temperature of 43°C (110°F).

15. May a partially cooked food be cooked more?

No. Although such food is edible in an emergency, further cooking will improve its quality and is therefore forbidden by the Torah according to most opinions. This applies whether the food becomes completely cooked or only slightly more cooked. Even if a food is almost fully cooked, it is a Torah transgression to cook it further. For this reason, it is forbidden to remove a pot of food from a fire and return it if even a small amount of the contents is not completely cooked.

16. May a fully cooked food be cooked more?

Yes. Even if additional cooking will improve the taste of the food this is not considered a significant change, and it is not included in the *melacha* of bishul. This rule is known as: *Ein bishul achar bishul* (cooking after cooking is not forbidden). For example, cold boiled carrots may be added to a pot of soup after it has been removed from the fire. Nevertheless, there are Rabbinical restrictions on how this may be done known as *chazara*. The details of these laws will be discussed in Chapter Ten.

17. When is food called fully cooked?

When the food is sufficiently well cooked that most people would be happy to eat it.

18. May one hard boil a soft boiled egg?

Opinions differ whether one may heat up a soft boiled egg if it will become hard boiled. Therefore, it is preferable not to do this. For example, to heat it on the cover of a pot or inside a hot pot off the fire.

Summary for Foods

19. What are all the stages of cooking for foods?

1. From cold until warm (less than *yad soledes bo*): Permitted, but only in a place where it cannot reach *yad soledes bo*.

2. From warm until hot: Forbidden Rabbinically.

3. From hot until it is partially cooked (*ma'achal ben drusai*): Forbidden by the Torah.

4. From partially cooked to fully cooked: Forbidden by the Torah.

5. Beyond fully cooked: Permitted, but subject to the restrictions of *chazara*.

Liquids

20. How does bishul apply to a liquid?

It is important to distinguish between a cold raw liquid and a cold cooked liquid. A cold raw liquid means one that has never been cooked, such as fresh water. A cold cooked liquid means one that was previously boiled but has gone cold, such as cold soup.

21. What are the laws for a cold raw liquid?

The Torah *melacha* of bishul is transgressed when a cold raw liquid is heated to *yad soledes bo* since such a change is considered to be significant. This is comparable to cooking a food from raw until *ma'achal ben drusai*. Compare Question 9.

22. May one warm up a cold raw liquid?

Yes, but only in a place where it is impossible for it to become hot. It is forbidden to put it even for a moment in a place where it can become hot since one might forget about it and allow it to get hot. Compare Question 12. For example:

• One must not put fresh orange juice on top of an urn to warm up if it could become hot there.

• One must not put a damp towel or garment on a hot radiator to dry if it could become hot there since this would cook the absorbed moisture. Compare Question 80.

23. May one stand next to a hot radiator while wearing damp clothes?

No, since this would cause cooking to the absorbed moisture. See also Question 338.

24. May a hot raw liquid be heated until it boils?

No. The change of temperature from *yad soledes bo* to boiling is significant, and therefore this is forbidden by the Torah. For example, a person filled a kettle with cold water and placed it on the blech just before Shabbos (see Question 193). He must not later move it closer to the flame in order to boil fully even after it has reached *yad soledes bo*.

25. What are the laws of reboiling a cooked liquid?

• If the cooked liquid has gone cold, it is forbidden to reboil it (*yeish bishul achar bishul*).

• If the cooked liquid is still reasonably warm, it is permitted to reboil it (*ein bishul achar bishul*). For example, a kettle of boiling water was placed on the blech before Shabbos. One may later move it closer to the flame to reboil it if it is still reasonably warm.

Note: *Sephardim* have stricter rules.

26. What is meant by reasonably warm?

It means that most people would enjoy drinking it if they wanted to drink something hot. This is slightly below *yad soledes bo*. For example, a bowl of soup was ladled out of a pot but was not drunk. One may return it to the pot (not on the fire) if it is still reasonably warm.

27. What if the cooked liquid went cold but was then made warm?

It is forbidden to reboil such liquid. Although it was made warm, the laws of bishul apply to it since it was previously cold. A warm cooked liquid may only be reboiled if it was previously hot and has not cooled down completely. In the above example, if the bowl of soup went cold it may not be returned to the pot by first adding a ladleful of hot soup to make it warm. Stated briefly, a warm cooked liquid may be reboiled if it is on its way down (from hot) but not if it is on its way up (from cold).

Summary for Liquids

28. What are all the stages of cooking for liquids?

1. From cold until warm: Permitted, but only in a place where it cannot reach *yad soledes bo*.

2. From warm until hot: Forbidden by the Torah.

3. From hot until boiling: Forbidden by the Torah.

4. Reboiling a boiled liquid: Permitted if still reasonably warm, but subject to the restrictions of *chazara*.

Boiling and Baking

29. May a baked food be baked more?

Yes. Just as a fully cooked food may be cooked more (see Question 16), a baked food may be baked more. This rule is known as: *Ein afiya achar afiya* (baking after baking is not forbidden). However, the restrictions of *chazara* still apply (see Chapter Ten). E.g., a challah may be heated up on top of an urn even if it reaches *yad soledes bo* and becomes more crispy. According to some opinions, one may not heat up slices of bread to make toast since this is a significant change of taste.

30. May a baked food be boiled?

No, since this causes a significant change to the taste of the food. This rule is known as: *Yeish bishul achar afiya* (boiling after baking is forbidden). For example: baked croutons may not be added to a pot of hot soup. See also Questions 70, 97, and 150.

Note: *Sephardim* have more lenient rules.

31. May a boiled food be baked?

This is forbidden only if the food is subjected to an intense heat that will impart a roasted flavor. This rule is known as: *Yeish afiya achar bishul* (baking after boiling is forbidden). For example, a pot of cholent was removed from the blech and served. If all the liquid has been poured off, it is forbidden to return the remaining food to the blech since it will begin to roast there. (This applies even if the pot was held all the time.)

32. What if there is still a small amount of liquid in the pot?

One may return the pot to the blech even if the liquid is likely to evaporate and the food will begin to roast. This is because at the time of placement on the fire the action is defined as boiling.

33. Why is roasting considered like baking?

Any form of dry cooking with no or very little liquid is categorized as baking. In contrast, any form of cooking with liquid is categorized as boiling.

Note: The place of cooking is irrelevant. It is possible to boil foods in an oven and bake foods on the stove.

34. How is frying categorized?

• If only a minimal amount of oil is used to prevent the food from burning, it is considered as baking.

• If more oil than that is used, it is considered as boiling. Even frying in a shallow layer of oil is included in this category.

35. How is pot roast categorized?

It is considered as boiled since liquid oozes out of the food during the cooking, and the food continues to cook in this liquid.

36. What are examples of each category?

• Boiled foods include: boiled or fried meat, chicken, fish, and vegetables; doughnuts; fried croutons.

• Baked foods include: bread, matzo, cookies, cake; meat, chicken, and fish roasted on a spit or grilled; kugel; pancakes fried in little or no oil.

37. May a cold boiled food be heated up on top of a pot on the fire?

Yes. Although this type of heat is dry and is equivalent to baking, it is permitted because the food will not change its taste significantly even if becomes very hot.

Note: If spices were added to a food after it was boiled, one must not reheat it on a pot on the fire. Since spices are raw, one must not heat them to *yad soledes bo* in this manner (see Question 81). For example, cooked chickpeas to which pepper was added.

38. May a cold food be heated on an upturned pan on the blech?

• A cold baked food may be heated by this method according to many opinions (see Question 280).

• A cold boiled food may be heated by this method according to many opinions provided one takes care that it does not start to roast due to the intense heat.

39. What if the food is wet?

See Question 84.

40. What if a food was both boiled and then baked before Shabbos?

- It is permitted to bake it on Shabbos since its present baked taste will not be changed.
- It is forbidden to boil it in a *kli rishon* but permitted to put it in a *kli sheini* (contrast Question 30).

For example, lokshen kugel is made by boiling and then baking noodles. It may be heated on Shabbos above a pot on the fire or by placing it in a *kli sheini* but not in a *kli rishon*. Similarly, if a pan of lokshen kugel on the fire is drying out, it is forbidden to pour hot water over it.

41. May one add hot water to a pot of cholent that is drying out?

Yes, this is permitted even if the food has dried out completely. See also Questions 242-244.

42. What if a food was baked and then boiled?

- It is permitted to put it in a *kli rishon* (off the fire) since its present boiled taste will not be changed.
- It is forbidden to heat it near the intense heat of a fire until its taste changes significantly.

For example, kneidels are made by boiling baked matzo meal. They may be put into a pot of hot soup (off the fire). They may be heated on an upturned pan on the blech if one takes care that they do not start to roast.

Summary

Type of Food	Near Fire	In *kli rishon* off the fire	In *kli sheini*
Boiled	✗	✓	✓
Baked	✓	✗	✗
Boiled and Baked	✓	✗	✓
Baked and Boiled	✗	✓	✓
Type of Liquid			
Boiled, cold	✗	✗	✓[1]
Boiled, still warm	✓	✓	✓

[1] See Question 96.

Chapter Two

Hastening the Cooking

43. What is meant by hastening the cooking?

Under certain conditions, it is permitted to leave raw or not fully cooked food on a fire at the onset of Shabbos and allow it to finish cooking of its own accord (see Chapter Nine). However, it is forbidden on Shabbos to do anything to the food that will help it to finish cooking sooner. Aside from the obvious prohibition of raising the flame, there are four actions that are forbidden:

- Moving the pot closer to the flame (or from a small flame to a larger one).
- Covering the pot.
- Stirring the food.
- Removing some of the food.

The first three activities are Torah prohibitions since they directly hasten the cooking. The fourth is forbidden Rabbinically since this affects the remaining food only indirectly.

Note: Due to these restrictions, it is advisable to ensure that all foods left on the fire are fully cooked before Shabbos (see Question 200).

44. Do these rules also apply to liquids?

Yes. If a cold liquid was placed on a fire before Shabbos, it is forbidden to cause it to boil faster by doing any of the above actions. For example, one must not remove water from an urn on Shabbos before it has fully boiled.

45. May one remove the cover of a pot?

Yes, since this does not hasten the cooking but rather slows it down. However, one must be extremely careful not to return the cover if any ingredient in the pot is not fully cooked. This could be relevant when cholent is set up raw just before Shabbos, and one later wishes to inspect the food to see how it is cooking.

46. May one replace the cover if it was only raised slightly?

No. Raising the cover even only slightly slows down the cooking somewhat, and replacing the cover then hastens the cooking again.

47. May one place a cloth over the pot cover?

No, since this insulates the heat more and hastens the cooking.

48. May one place a cooked food on the pot cover?

One may usually heat up a cooked food by placing it on the cover of a pot on the fire (see Question 276). However, one may not do this if the contents of the pot are not fully cooked since it might hasten the cooking.

49. Could this restriction apply to food in an oven?

Yes. If a pot of food in an oven is not fully cooked, one may open the oven door. However, it is then forbidden to close the door again since this is equivalent to adding another cover to the pot.

50. What if the oven is off?

As long as the oven is hot the food will still continue to cook, and it is therefore forbidden to close the door.

51. Do these restrictions apply to a pot that was removed from the fire?

Yes. A pot of hot food that is not fully cooked will still continue to cook from its own heat even after it has been removed from the fire. Therefore, it is forbidden to stir the food, remove some, or cover the pot.

52. How could such food be served?

One may slowly pour it directly from the pot into the plate.

Fully Cooked Food

53. Do any restrictions apply to fully cooked hot food?

A distinction must be made between a pot that is directly on top of the fire (even if covered with a blech) and one that is not on top of the fire. If the pot is not on top of the fire, it is permitted to stir the food, remove some, and cover the pot. This applies whether the pot is totally removed from the fire (e.g. on a countertop or table) or it is on the blech but not on top of the fire. It might also be permitted to move it onto the area of the fire, but this is subject to the laws of *chazara* (see Chapter Ten).

54. What if the pot is on top of the fire?

- It is permitted to move it from a small flame to a larger one.
- It is permitted to cover the pot.
- It is forbidden to stir the food.
- It is usually forbidden to remove some food.

55. When is it permitted to remove some food?

In the following cases:

- If the pot contains only dry solids, one may remove pieces while it is on top of the fire. E.g. kugel, pieces of meat or chicken.

- Water may be taken from an urn or pot by opening the faucet or by scooping out from the top. See also Question 265.
- According to some opinions, one may take out from the top layer of food in a pot if one is careful not to cause any stirring. Ideally, the pot should be moved from the fire before taking out any food.

56. May one ladle clear soup from a pot on top of the fire?

Opinions differ whether the leniency of water also applies to other clear liquids such as soup.

57. May food be removed from a pot that is too heavy to move away from the fire?

No. If the pot is too heavy to move single-handed, one should get another person to help.

58. What if a pot is only partially on the flame?

It is considered as on the flame. Therefore, if one wishes to stir or ladle out the food, one should move the pot completely away from the area of the flame. See also Question 292.

59. Is a pot on a hotplate considered on the flame?

Yes. Since the electric element runs across the hotplate, all areas are considered above the flame. It is therefore forbidden to stir or ladle out food from a pot on a hotplate. The same applies to a crockpot.

60. What if a pot of fully cooked food contains chicken bones?

If a pot of cholent contains pieces of chicken, it is common for the bones to be hard in the evening but soft and edible by the morning. Opinions differ whether the four actions discussed in this chapter are permitted in the evening since they will hasten the cooking of the bones. According to many opinions, this depends on whether any member of the family is interested in eating the bones. If there is such an interest, it is forbidden in the evening to move the pot closer to the flame, to cover or stir it, or to remove some food. If there is no such interest, all the actions are permitted if the pot is not on the flame. According to some opinions, if the chicken has been cooking for four hours the bones are considered as cooked and the restrictions do not apply.

Summary

	Not fully cooked	Fully cooked, on the flame	Fully cooked, not on the flame
To move closer to the flame	✗	✓	✓[1]
To cover	✗	✓	✓
To stir	✗	✗	✓
To remove some food	✗	✗[2]	✓

[1] Subject to the laws of *chazara*

[2] Except dry solids and water

Chapter Three
Kli Rishon

61. What is meant by a *kli rishon*?

Literally this means a first vessel. It refers to a pot or pan of food or liquid that has been heated by any type of fire such as a stove, oven, hotplate, crockpot, or electric urn. A *kli rishon* is called so even after it has been removed from the fire.

62. What if the pot was only indirectly heated by fire?

It is still called a *kli rishon*. For example:
- A pot placed on a hot part of the blech not on the flame.
- A pot placed above another pot on a fire.

63. What is the significance of a *kli rishon*?

As explained previously (see Question 6), it is a Torah prohibition to cook food directly or indirectly through fire. The most common application of this is the severe prohibition to put any type of raw food or liquid into a *kli rishon* whether it is on or off the fire. For example, one must not do the following:
- Add spices to a pot of soup, vegetables, cholent, etc. on the kitchen table or counter.
- Add cold water or ice cubes to such a pot.

64.   May one open a hot water faucet?

This is usually forbidden. The hot water tank is a *kli rishon* since it is heated by an electric element. Opening the faucet causes cold water to enter the tank, and this water will cook immediately on contact with the hot water (compare Question 8). One may open the faucet only if the water is less than *yad soledes bo*, the boiler is switched off, and there are no solar panels.

65.   What if one has a mixer tap?

Extreme care must be taken to ensure that it is turned fully towards the cold faucet before opening it. It is forbidden to allow a mixture of hot and cold water to be released together since this will also cause cooking.

66.   What if one accidentally opened the hot water faucet?

Assuming the boiler is off, the rules are as follows:
- If the water is very hot, one may close the faucet.
- If the water is not so hot, opinions differ whether one may close the faucet. One should preferably hint to a gentile to close it, if possible. One may leave the water running until it is less than *yad soledes bo* and then close it.

67. May one add water to a hot water vaporizer?

- It is forbidden to add cold water since it will become cooked. This applies even to cold cooked water.

- It is forbidden to add even hot water if this entails removal of the heating unit since that shuts off the machine.
- If water could be added without disconnecting the unit, opinions differ whether one may add hot water. A rav should be consulted.

68. May one add water to a cold water vaporizer?

Yes, provided this can be done without disconnecting the unit.

69. May one put a cold cooked food into a *kli rishon* on the fire?

No. Although the *melacha* of bishul does not apply in this case (see Question 16), nevertheless, *Chazal* forbid doing this since it resembles the act of cooking. Details of this prohibition are discussed in Chapter Ten.

70. May one put a cold cooked food into a *kli rishon* off the fire?

- Baked or roasted foods are forbidden due to the rule of *yeish bishul achar afiya* (see Question 30). For example, one must not put a piece of roast meat or chicken or baked croutons into a pot of soup.
- Boiled foods are permitted due to the rule of *ein bishul achar bishul* (see Question 16). For example, one may put a piece of boiled meat or chicken or boiled vegetables into a pot of soup.

71. What if the boiled food is wet?

•   If the moisture is a raw liquid, the food must not be put into a *kli rishon* since the liquid will become cooked. E.g. cooked noodles rinsed with fresh water.

•   If the moisture is a cooked liquid, the food may be put into a *kli rishon* off the fire provided there is not a significant amount of liquid. E.g. kneidels, noodles drained of the cooking water or rinsed with cooked water.

72. What if the boiled food is covered with congealed fat?

One may put it into a *kli rishon* off the fire since its initial form is a solid food for which recooking is permitted. For example, to put a piece of meat or chicken with congealed fat into a pot of soup. See also Question 85.

73. May one add sugar to a *kli rishon* off the fire?

Although sugar is cooked during its manufacture, one should preferably avoid adding it to a *kli rishon*. According to some opinions, it is treated like a liquid for which recooking is forbidden (see Question 25). Since it dissolves completely and disappears in the hot liquid, it is treated like its final state, i.e. a liquid. The same applies to other cooked powders. This is in contrast to congealed fat (see previous question), which is still recognizable after it melts in the hot liquid and is therefore treated like its original state, i.e. a food.

74. May one add salt to a *kli rishon* off the fire?

There are two types of salt - raw and cooked. Salt that is made by evaporating seawater in the sun is considered to be raw, whereas salt that is made by boiling seawater is cooked. Mined salt is also cooked.

• Raw salt should preferably not be put into a *kli rishon* off the fire.

• One should preferably avoid putting cooked salt into a *kli rishon* off the fire since it dissolves (compare previous question).

Note: All salt in *Eretz Yisroel* is raw. Production methods are different in other parts of the world.

75. May one add sugar or salt to a *kli rishon* containing only dry food?

• Raw salt should preferably not be added.

• Sugar and cooked salt may be added since they do not dissolve into a liquid but become absorbed in the dry food. For example, adding them to a pan of kugel or a pot of dry cholent off the fire.

76. What are the rules for adding a liquid to a *kli rishon* off the fire?

• All raw liquids are forbidden. E.g. water.

• All cold boiled liquids are forbidden. E.g. cold soup, cold boiled water.

• A liquid that was boiled and is cooling down may be added to a *kli rishon* if the liquid is still reasonably warm (see Question 26). E.g. warm soup.

77. May one use a wet soup ladle to serve soup from a *kli rishon*?

• If the ladle is wet from rinsing with fresh water, this is forbidden. Therefore, the ladle must be wiped dry before it is used.

• If the ladle is wet from soup that is still warm, it is permitted. This commonly happens when ladling several bowls of soup consecutively, and it is unnecessary to dry the ladle between uses.

• If the ladle is wet from soup that has gone cold, one should shake off the droplets before resuming use. The remaining moisture is negligible, and it is unnecessary to wipe the ladle dry.

78. Should one be concerned about condensed droplets on the underneath of a pot cover?

Care should be taken to avoid such droplets falling back into the pot after they have gone cold. This applies whether the pot is still on the fire or has been removed from the fire. Therefore, if the cover has been taken off the pot for sufficient time to allow the droplets to cool off, one should shake them off before returning the cover. The remaining moisture is negligible, and it is unnecessary to wipe the cover dry. If the droplets are still warm, the cover may be returned without shaking it.

79. Can the outside of a *kli rishon* cause bishul?

Yes. For example, when taking a pot from the fire one should avoid placing it on a wet surface since the hot pot would cook the moisture.

80. May one place a pot on a damp cloth?

No, since this also causes the moisture in the cloth to cook. In addition, one transgresses the *melacha* of laundering (*melabein*) since the combination of heat with moisture cleans the cloth. Similarly, one must not wear wet oven gloves when removing a *kli rishon* from the fire.

81. May one place a raw food on the cover of a *kli rishon*?

No, since the food could reach *yad soledes bo* and start to cook. E.g. an apple or carrot. See also Question 12.

82. May one place cold liquid on the cover of a *kli rishon*?

No, since the liquid could reach *yad soledes bo*. E.g. a bottle of cold baby formula. See also Question 22. This applies also to a cold cooked liquid.

83. May one defrost a frozen cooked food on the cover of a *kli rishon*?

Yes, but one must first remove any ice since it is forbidden to allow ice to reach *yad soledes bo*. E.g. frozen challah, cake, or kugel.

84. May one heat a wet cooked food on the cover of a *kli rishon*?

- If the moisture is a raw liquid, it is forbidden.
- If the moisture is a cooked liquid, it is permitted provided there is not a significant amount of liquid.

Compare Question 71.

85. What if the cooked food is covered with congealed fat?

- It is permitted to heat it on the cover of a *kli rishon* if there is not a significant amount of fat. This means that the melted fat will remain on the food and will not become a separate liquid.
- It is forbidden if there is so much fat that it will become a separate liquid when melted. This is due to a Rabbinic restriction called *molid* - transforming the state of a substance from solid to liquid.

86. May one heat a doughnut on the cover of a *kli rishon*?

- It is permitted if there is no jelly inside, or only a small amount, or a significant amount of thick jelly.
- If there is a significant amount of liquidy jelly inside, it is forbidden. Although the jelly is cooked in the manufacture, it is forbidden to recook it. See Question 25.

87. Can an empty *kli rishon* cause bishul?

Yes. For example, one should avoid putting an empty hot pot inside a wet sink since the heat of the pot will cook the drops of water. If there is a large amount of water in the sink that will not reach *yad soledes bo*, one may put the pot there.

88. May one pour cold water into an empty *kli rishon*?

There are two issues involved when doing this: bishul and *hachana* (preparing for after Shabbos).

• Regarding bishul, one may not pour a small amount of water into an empty *kli rishon* if it will reach *yad soledes bo*. There is no problem of bishul if a large amount of water is poured in at one go.

• Regarding *hachana*, opinions differ whether one may fill a dirty pot with water to prevent the leftover food from hardening, which will facilitate washing up on *motzai Shabbos*. However, one may leave the empty pot in the sink and allow it to fill up with water incidentally as he washes his hands or uses the sink for other purposes throughout Shabbos.

89. What if a *kli rishon* has cooled down to below *yad soledes bo*?

Once the temperature is below the lowest figure for *yad soledes bo* (43°C; 110°F) it is no longer called a *kli rishon*, and it is incapable of cooking anything. Therefore, all types of foods or liquids may be put into it.

Chapter Four
Kli Sheini

90. What is meant by a *kli sheini*?

Literally this means a second vessel. It refers to a hot liquid that was poured directly from a *kli rishon* into a container. For example: a cup of hot water filled from an urn; a soup tureen filled directly from a pot. Regarding transferred foods, see Chapter Eight; regarding liquids transferred with a ladle, see Chapter Seven.

91. Can a *kli sheini* cause bishul?

Yes, but not to all types of foods and liquids. The power of a *kli sheini* to cook is considerably less than that of a *kli rishon* since the cold walls of the container remove the intense heat of the liquid and cause it to cool down quickly.

92. Which items can cook in a *kli sheini*?

All foods and liquids are divided into two categories:
- *Kalei habishul* - those that cook easily.
- *Kashei habishul* - those that cook with difficulty.

The rule is that *kalei habishul* items must not be put into a *kli sheini* since they can become cooked there. Items that are *kashei habishul* may be put into a *kli sheini*.

93.   Which foods are *kashei habishul*?

Unfortunately, over the course of time it has become unknown which foods are *kashei habishul*. However, it is agreed that the following two items are *kashei habishul* and may therefore be put into a *kli sheini*: pieces of ginger and cinnamon sticks. All other raw foods are suspect to be *kalei habishul* and should not be put into a *kli sheini*. For example:

- Powdered spices, including ginger and cinnamon.
- Onions.
- Slice of lemon.
- Tea, cocoa.

94.   May one put raw salt in a *kli sheini*?

According to most opinions, salt is *kashei habishul* and may be put into a *kli sheini*. However, it is praiseworthy to refrain due to the minority opinion that salt is *kalei habishul*. See also Question 74.

95.   Which liquids are *kashei habishul*?

Water and oil are definitely *kashei habishul* and may be put into a *kli sheini*. Opinions differ regarding other liquids, and it is preferable not to put other raw liquids into a *kli sheini*. For example: fresh orange juice, fresh lemon juice, unpasteurized wine and grape juice.

96.   What if a liquid is pasteurized?

All pasteurized or cooked liquids may be put into a *kli sheini*. For example: milk, orange juice, lemon juice.
Note: One may assume that all manufactured drinks are pasteurized unless the label states otherwise.

97. May one put a baked or roasted food in a *kli sheini*?

According to *Ashkenazic* custom, one should not put a baked or roasted food in a *kli sheini*. This is because the baking or roasting process makes the food *kalei habishul*. Although the food has already been baked, it is subject to the rule of *yeish bishul achar afiya* (see Question 30). For example: bread, matzo, biscuits, cookies, baked croutons, roast meat and chicken, roasted coffee granules or powder.

98. May one put a cooked powder in a *kli sheini*?

Yes. Although one should preferably not put a cooked powder in a *kli rishon* (see Question 73), one may put it in a *kli sheini*. For example: sugar, cooked salt, instant coffee, instant tea granules.

99. May one put artificial sweeteners in a *kli sheini*?

Only if one is certain that all the ingredients have been cooked. However, it has been ascertained that some sweeteners contain raw ingredients, and it is often difficult to obtain the relevant information about any particular brand. Therefore, it is recommended to use them only in a *kli shelishi*. The same applies to dehydrated soup mixes, instant cocoa powder, and baby formula.

100. Is it preferable not to put instant coffee into a *kli sheini*?

Yes. Although instant coffee may be put into a *kli sheini*, some opinions advise one to use only a *kli shelishi*. Several reasons have been suggested:
- The coffee beans might not have been fully cooked.
- The powder is dried after cooking and this might be considered as roasting, making subsequent boiling questionable.
- Other ingredients might be mixed into the coffee that are forbidden in a *kli sheini*.

101. Is it preferable not to put instant tea in a *kli sheini*?

- If the tea does not contain added flavorings, there is no reason to require a *kli shelishi*.
- If the tea contains flavorings (e.g. lemon), it is preferable to put it into a *kli shelishi* in case the flavoring is raw.

102. May one put honey in a *kli sheini*?

No, since all types of honey are not cooked but are only processed with slight heat. It may be put in a *kli shelishi*.

103. Is a Thermos filled from a *kli rishon* called a *kli sheini*?

Yes. Although the liquid in a Thermos retains its heat for a long time, the original intense heat is removed as soon as it makes contact with the cold walls.

104. What if the walls of a *kli sheini* are pre-heated?

If a cup is filled with hot water from an urn, emptied out, and refilled with hot water, it is still considered a *kli sheini*. Since the walls of the cup were not heated by fire, they do not retain their heat for long, and therefore they have the same effect as cold walls.

105. What if an empty container is pre-heated on a blech or hotplate?

It is considered to be a *kli rishon*.

106. What if the contents of a *kli sheini* are returned to an empty hot *kli rishon*?

They continue to be considered a *kli sheini*.

107. What if a *kli sheini* is extremely hot?

According to some opinions, if a *kli sheini* is so intensely hot that one's hand would be scalded from it, it is considered like a *kli rishon*. This temperature is called *yad nichveis bo*. E.g. a cup of hot water immediately after it is filled from an urn. It is preferable to be strict and follow this opinion.

108. What is the temperature of *yad nichveis bo*?

It is difficult to give a figure, but it is very close to boiling point.

109. For how long could a *kli sheini* remain *yad nichveis bo*?

Only for a very short time.

110. What are the laws of a *kli sheini* that is *yad nichveis bo*?

• One should not put into it items that are strictly forbidden in a *kli rishon*. For example, cold water or ice. Therefore, if one wishes to prepare a bowl of warm water for washing dirty dishes or for bathing and fills a bowl from the urn for this purpose, he should not immediately add cold water to it. Rather, he should wait for a short time until the hot water is not scorching hot before adding the cold water. See also Questions 132 and 335.

• One may put into it items that are forbidden in a *kli rishon* due to a custom or a stringency. For example: adding sugar, tea essence, or pasteurised lemon juice to a scorching *kli sheini* cup of water.

111. May one warm up a baby's bottle by standing it in a *kli sheini* of hot water?

This is equivalent to pouring the contents of the bottle into the *kli sheini*. Therefore, the rules are as follows:

• If all the contents of the bottle have been cooked previously, this is permitted.

• If there is an uncooked item in the bottle, this is forbidden unless the only uncooked item is cold water (see Question 99).

112. What if the *kli sheini* is *yad nichveis bo*?

It is forbidden to warm up the bottle in it unless every item in the bottle is cooked, including the water.

113. What if one takes care that the contents of the bottle do not become *yad soledes bo*?

The rules remain the same since it is forbidden to warm up a raw item in a place where it could become *yad soledes bo* (see Questions 12 and 22).

114. What if a *kli sheini* has cooled down to below *yad soledes bo*?

It is incapable of cooking anything, and therefore all types of foods and liquids may be put into it, including *kalei habishul*.

Chapter Five
Kli Shelishi

115. What is meant by a *kli shelishi*?

Literally this means a third vessel. It refers to a hot liquid that was poured from a *kli sheini* into another container. For example, a jug was filled with hot water from an urn and poured into a cup. The jug is a *kli sheini* and the cup is a *kli shelishi*.

116. Can a *kli shelishi* cause bishul?

Yes, but only to a very few items that can cook extremely easily. Therefore, all types of foods and liquids may be put into a *kli shelishi* except the following:

- Raw eggs.
- Tea-bags, tea-leaves, mint leaves, etc.
- Salted fish, e.g. herring.
- Small tender fish, e.g. sardines.

117. What if a *kli shelishi* is exceedingly hot?

The rules are the same. The stringency regarding *yad nichveis bo* applies only to a *kli sheini* but not to a *kli shelishi*.

118. What if a *kli shelishi* is less than *yad soledes bo*?

It is incapable of cooking anything, and therefore all types of foods and liquids may be put into it, including those mentioned above.

119. Is there a concept of *kli reviyi*?

No. If a *kli shelishi* is poured into another container, it is still considered a *kli shelishi* as long as it is *yad soledes bo*.

120. May a used tea-bag be put into a *kli shelishi*?

Yes. Since the tea leaves were cooked before Shabbos when placed in a *kli sheini*, they will not cook any further when put into a *kli shelishi*.

121. What are the recommended ways to make tea on Shabbos?

One simple method is to use instant tea granules, which are considered a cooked food and may be put into a *kli sheini* (see also Question 144). One should not pour the hot water directly from the urn onto the granules (see Question 129). Alternatively, one can make a concentrated tea essence before Shabbos using tea-bags (or leaves) and hot water. This may be added on Shabbos to hot water in a *kli sheini* (see also Question 145). One should not pour hot water directly onto the cold essence (see Question 129).

122. Should the tea essence be kept warm throughout Shabbos?

This is not necessary. However, if one did keep it warm (e.g. on top of an urn), one may pour hot water directly from the urn onto warm essence in a cup. According to some opinions, one should use this essence only as one uses cold essence.

123. May the tea-bags be left in the essence?

Yes, but one must not squeeze the tea-bags in order to extract more flavor. In addition, one may only use the essence as long as there is a layer of liquid covering the tea-bags. When there is little or no liquid left, it is forbidden to try to pour out the essence since this involves the *melacha* of borer (see Guidelines to Borer, Question 190).

124. May one remove the tea-bags on Shabbos?

Yes, but one must put them down immediately. It is forbidden to hold the tea-bags above the pot to allow the drips to fall in since this involves the *melacha* of borer (see Guidelines to Borer, Question 308). It is permitted to remove the tea-bags with a spoon.

125. May one make tea essence on Shabbos?

Yes, by soaking tea-bags in cold or lukewarm water (i.e. less than *yad soledes bo*). The resulting essence may then be added to hot water in a *kli sheini* even after it has gone cold.

126. May one put coffee granules or powder in a *kli shelishi*?

•   Instant coffee is usually pre-cooked and may be put in a *kli shelishi*. See also Question 100.

•   Opinions differ whether non-instant coffee (sometimes called Turkish coffee or black coffee) may be put into a *kli shelishi*.

Chapter Six

Iruy

127. What is meant by *iruy*?

Literally this means pouring. It refers to the pouring of a hot liquid onto a food or another liquid. We shall discuss two types of *iruy*:

- *Iruy kli rishon* - pouring from a *kli rishon* (even off the fire).
- *Iruy kli sheini* - pouring from a *kli sheini*.

Iruy Kli Rishon

128. What is the law of *iruy kli rishon*?

It has the power to cook like the *kli rishon* itself. Therefore, it is forbidden to pour from a *kli rishon* onto any item that one may not put into a *kli rishon*. This includes the following:

- All raw foods (see Question 63).
- Baked and roasted foods (see Question 30).
- All cold liquids, whether raw or cooked (see Question 76).

129. What are practical examples?

• If one wishes to make a hot drink in a *kli sheini* using a cooked powder such as instant coffee or instant tea, one should first pour the water from the urn into an empty cup and then add the powder. One should not put the powder into the empty cup and then add the hot water. See also Question 144.

• If one wishes to make a cup of tea in a *kli sheini* using cold tea essence, one should first pour the hot water into an empty cup and then add the essence. One should not put the essence into the empty cup and then add the hot water. See also Question 145.

• One must not pour hot water from an urn onto a slice of lemon.

• One must not pour hot gravy from a pot onto raw vegetables.

130. May one pour hot water from an urn into a wet cup?

• If the moisture is from a raw liquid, this is forbidden, and the cup must be dried first. For example, a cup that was washed with cold water.

• If the moisture is from a cooked liquid, it is sufficient to shake out any droplets, and the remaining moisture may then be ignored. For example, a cup that was used previously to transfer hot water from the urn to a *kli shelishi*. Compare Question 71.

131. May one fill a hot water bottle from an urn?

• If the bottle is wet inside from previous use, one should shake out any droplets and may then fill it from the urn.

• If the inside is wet from cold water that was previously added, it is forbidden to fill it from an urn. Rather, one should fill a jug from the urn and pour the hot water from the jug into the bottle (see Question 136).

The same applies to filling a Thermos from an urn.

132. May one add a small amount of hot water from an urn to a large amount of cold liquid?

Yes, provided the final temperature of the mixture is less than *yad soledes bo*. In this situation, the hot water is unable to cook the cold liquid since the hot is overpowered by the cold. For example:

• A person needs warm water for bathing or for washing dirty dishes. He may fill a bowl with cold water and add a small amount of hot water from the urn. See also Question 110.

• A person wishes to drink warm orange juice. He may add a small amount of hot water from the urn to a cup of cold juice.

In any event, one must take care not to allow the mixture to reach *yad soledes bo* by adding too much hot water.

133. May one pour water from an urn over a baby bottle containing cold liquid?

This is permitted provided the contents of the bottle are items that may be put into a *kli sheini*. For example: cold water, pre-cooked powder, pasteurized juice. Although such ingredients are forbidden in a *kli rishon* and pouring from a *kli rishon* cooks like a *kli rishon*, nevertheless this procedure is permitted. The reason is because *iruy kli rishon* will cook with *kli rishon* power only the outer layer of the item. The inside of the item is considered to be cooked only with *kli sheini* power. In the case of a baby bottle, the bottle acts as the outer layer and does not allow the intense heat of the *kli rishon* water to reach the contents. This is permitted even if the contents reach *yad soledes bo*. Care should be taken to make sure that the outside of the bottle is dry.

134. What if there is a raw ingredient in the bottle?

This procedure is forbidden if there is a raw ingredient other than water, such as fresh juice or uncooked powder, since these may not be put into a *kli sheini*. Even if the intention is only to warm up the bottle, this is forbidden since it is possible for the contents to become *yad soledes bo*. Compare Questions 12 and 22.

135. May one add hot water from an urn to a hot drink made in a *kli sheini*?

It sometimes happens that a person makes a hot drink in a *kli sheini* and a little while later wishes to add more hot water to make it hotter. In most cases, one should not add the hot water directly from an urn. This is because most ingredients in a hot drink should not be subjected to *iruy kli rishon*; for example: instant coffee, instant tea, cold tea essence, sugar, milk. Although the ingredients have already become part of the hot drink in the *kli sheini*, nevertheless one should not make them even hotter through *iruy kli rishon*. Rather, one should add hot water from a *kli sheini* (see next section).

Iruy Kli Sheini

136. What is the law of *iruy kli sheini*?

It is considered equivalent to a *kli shelishi*. Therefore, it is permitted to pour from a *kli sheini* onto almost everything including raw foods and liquids. The only exceptions are those listed in Question 116.

137. What is a practical example?

If one wishes to make a hot drink using a raw ingredient and must therefore use a *kli shelishi*, it does not matter whether the hot water or the ingredient is put first into the cup. For example: one may pour hot *kli sheini* water onto fresh juice, instant cocoa, soup mix, or baby formula since this is equivalent to putting them into a *kli shelishi*.

138. What if the *kli sheini* is *yad nichveis bo*?

Pouring onto an item from a *kli sheini* that is *yad nichveis bo* is equivalent to putting the item into that *kli*. For example, one should not pour from a scorching hot *kli sheini* onto cold water. See Question 110.

139. May one pour hot chocolate over ice cream?

No, since the hot liquid will cook the raw eggs in the ice cream. Although manufactured ice cream contains pasteurized eggs, they are not considered cooked. One should not pour even from a *kli sheini* since eggs are forbidden in a *kli shelishi*. See also Question 177.

Tzoveya

140. What is *tzoveya*?

One of the thirty-nine forbidden *melachos* on Shabbos is *tzoveya* - dyeing. This usually refers to the coloring of objects and materials. Regarding foods and drinks, the following rules apply:

• If the color is added specifically to enhance the appearance of the food or drink, opinions differ whether it is permitted and it is therefore preferable not to do this.

• If the color is added to enhance the flavor of the food or drink, it is permitted. Nevertheless, it is praiseworthy to avoid doing this.

141. What is an example of coloring for appearance?

On the Seder night, it is preferable to drink red wine rather than white. If the white wine is of superior quality one may use it, but it is better to mix it with a little red wine. One should preferably pour the white wine into the red wine and not the reverse in order to avoid the issue of dyeing.

142. Why is it permitted to pour the white wine into the red?

Since the red wine is put into the cup first, the addition of white wine only causes the red color to be diluted. Although the white wine automatically turns red, the focus of the activity is on the item placed first, i.e. what happens to the red wine.

143. What is an example of coloring for flavor?

When concentrated syrup is diluted with water to make a drink of juice, the water becomes colored. Since the intention is for flavor, it is permitted to add either one to the other. Nevertheless, it is praiseworthy to add the water to the syrup rather than the reverse.

144. How does this apply to making a hot drink?

If one wishes to mix hot water with a powder such as instant coffee or instant tea, it is better to add the water to the powder than the reverse. Nevertheless, one must be very careful to avoid forbidden bishul on this account. Since one should not pour from a *kli rishon* onto any type of powder (see Question 128), the most praiseworthy method of making the hot drink is to pour from a *kli sheini* onto the powder. If one prefers to make it in a *kli sheini*, he should ignore the issue of *tzoveya* and put the powder into the water (see Question 129).

145. How does this apply to tea essence?

It is better to add hot water to the essence rather than the reverse. If the essence is kept constantly warm, one may pour even from a *kli rishon*, but if the essence is cold one must pour the hot water from a *kli sheini*. If one prefers to make it in a *kli sheini*, he should ignore the issue of *tzoveya* and pour the cold essence into the hot water. See Question 129.

Summary

	Warm Tea Essence	Cold Tea Essence, Instant Tea/Coffee	Cocoa, Soup Mix, Baby Formula
Iruy kli rishon	Praiseworthy	Forbidden	Forbidden
In *kli sheini*	Permitted	Permitted	Forbidden
Iruy kli sheini	Praiseworthy	Praiseworthy	Praiseworthy
In *kli shelishi*	Permitted	Permitted	Permitted

Chapter Seven
The Ladle

146. Is a ladle a *kli sheini*?

When one ladles a hot liquid such as soup from a *kli rishon* into a bowl, there is uncertainty whether the ladle qualifies to be a *kli sheini*. As explained earlier (Question 91), a typical *kli sheini* has cold walls that remove the intense heat of the liquid. This does not happen with a ladle since it is submerged in the hot *kli rishon*. On the other hand, the ladle does not qualify to be a *kli rishon* since it is not heated by fire (see Question 61). Accordingly, opinions differ regarding the status of the ladle. Some treat it like a *kli rishon* and therefore the bowl is a *kli sheini*, whereas others treat it like a *kli sheini* and the bowl is a *kli shelishi*.

147. What is the final ruling?

According to most opinions, the ladle is regarded as a *kli rishon* and the bowl as a *kli sheini*. However, if there are other factors in any particular case, one may treat the ladle as a *kli sheini* and the bowl as a *kli shelishi*.

148. May one put raw spices in a bowl of soup?

Raw spices should not be put into a *kli sheini* (see Question 93). Therefore, they should not be put into a bowl of soup that was ladled from a *kli rishon* since the bowl is considered a *kli sheini*.

149. May one put raw salt in a bowl of soup?

Yes. Although it is praiseworthy to refrain from putting raw salt in a *kli sheini* (see Question 94), nevertheless it is permitted according to most opinions. This factor allows one to regard the bowl of soup ladled from a *kli rishon* as a *kli shelishi*, thereby permitting one to add the raw salt according to all opinions.

150. May one put bread in a bowl of soup?

Yes. Although the *Ashkenazic* custom is to refrain from putting bread in a *kli sheini* (see Question 97), nevertheless this is only a stringency. This factor allows one to regard the bowl of soup ladled from a *kli rishon* as a *kli shelishi*, thereby permitting one to put in the bread. The same applies to other baked foods such as matzo and baked croutons.

151. May one pour from a ladle into a wet rinsed bowl?

No, a rinsed bowl must be wiped dry before ladling hot soup into it. Since the ladle is treated like a *kli rishon*, its *iruy* cooks with *kli rishon* power and is therefore forbidden on droplets of raw water (see Question 130). In this case there is no lenient factor that can allow one to consider the ladle to be a *kli sheini*.

152. May one pour from a ladle onto wet rinsed noodles?

No, since this is parallel to the previous question, and the *iruy* from the ladle will cook the raw water on the noodles. Rather, one should pour the soup first into the empty bowl and then add the noodles. This makes the soup a *kli sheini* in which one may put raw water (see Question 95).

153. May one pour from a ladle onto a cold cooked liquid?

Yes. Since the liquid is cooked, this is a lenient factor that allows the ladle to be treated as a *kli sheini*. Therefore, in the previous case if the noodles had been rinsed with cooked water, one may ladle the soup onto them. Similarly, if one desires a second bowl of soup, he may ladle the hot soup onto the cold remnants of soup in his bowl.

154. What if the ladle was left inside the *kli rishon* for some time?

The rules of the ladle remain the same as above provided the *kli rishon* was not on the fire. For example, a pot of soup was removed from the fire and put down on the kitchen table. When serving the soup one may leave the ladle inside the pot while not in use, and the laws of the ladle apply as explained above. Some people even prefer to leave the ladle inside the pot in order to avoid the problem of cold soup droplets (see Question 77).

155. Does a plastic ladle have the same rules as a metal one?

Yes. Although plastic does not conduct heat as well as metal, nevertheless the rules of a ladle are the same for all materials.

156. What if one ladles from a *kli rishon* on the fire?

This is usually forbidden since ladling causes stirring, which is forbidden on the fire (see Question 54). However, it is permitted in the following two cases:

- Water.
- Other liquids such as soup when the pot is on the blech not directly over the flame.

In these situations, if the ladle is left in the *kli rishon* for some time, the ladle is definitely a *kli rishon*. If the ladle is used regularly without leaving it in the *kli rishon*, it is correct to treat the ladle as a *kli rishon* without any leniences.

157. What if one ladles from a *kli sheini*?

Theoretically, the ladle should be treated as a *kli sheini*. However, this does not usually have any practical application since the *iruy* of a *kli sheini* is considered like a *kli shelishi*. This means that one may pour from the ladle onto almost anything (see Question 136). The bowl into which the ladle is poured is certainly a *kli shelishi*.

Chapter Eight
Davar Gush

158. What is meant by a *davar gush*?

This refers to a hot solid food that has been removed from a *kli rishon*. For example: a piece of meat, chicken, fish, kugel, or kishke, thick cholent, a potato, an egg, or a carrot.

159. What is the significance of a *davar gush*?

As explained in earlier chapters, when a hot liquid is transferred from a *kli rishon* to a *kli sheini*, it loses some of its power to cook. If it is transferred from a *kli sheini* to a *kli shelishi* it has even less power to cook. According to some opinions, these rules do not apply to a solid food. Unlike liquids, a hot solid food retains its intense heat even after it has been transferred several times since it has relatively little contact with the cold surface on which it lies. Therefore, it is capable of cooking anything it touches with *kli rishon* power no matter how many times it is moved. According to other opinions, a solid food has the same laws as a liquid, and it changes to a *kli sheini* and *kli shelishi* with successive transfers.

160. What is the final ruling?

A *davar gush* should be regarded as a *kli rishon*. However, if other lenient factors are involved in any particular case, one may treat the *davar gush* like a *kli sheini* after one transfer and like a *kli shelishi* after two transfers.

161. When does it lose its power to cook?

When every part of the food including the inside is less than *yad soledes bo*.

162. Are small pieces of food considered a *davar gush*?

- If the pieces are stuck together in a lump, they are a *davar gush*. For example: a clump of rice or noodles.
- If the pieces remain separate, they are not a *davar gush*. For example: loose rice or farfel, chick peas.

163. What if a *davar gush* is inside liquid?

The food is treated according to the rules of the surrounding liquid: if the liquid is *kli sheini*, so is the food inside it; and if the liquid is *kli shelishi*, so is the food inside it. For example, if a pot of chicken soup with carrots is poured into a serving tureen, the soup and the carrots are both *kli sheini*.

164. What if a carrot is removed from the pot?

It is a *davar gush*. Although it was inside soup in the pot, it was a *kli rishon* there and does not lose its power when removed.

165. What if a carrot is removed from the tureen?

It is not a *davar gush*. Once it is in liquid in the *kli sheini* it loses its power of *kli rishon* and is no longer considered a *davar gush*.

166. What if a *davar gush* is partially submerged in a *kli sheini*?

The part that is submerged is considered a *kli sheini*, but the part that is exposed is considered a *davar gush* and has the laws of a *kli rishon*. For example, a liquidy cholent containing large pieces of meat or potatoes.

167. May one put raw spices on a *davar gush*?

This should be avoided.

168. May one put salt on a *davar gush*?

- Cooked salt is permitted. See Question 75.
- Regarding raw salt, one should not put it on a *davar gush* that has been transferred once (i.e. to a *kli sheini*), but one may put it on a *davar gush* that has been transferred twice (i.e. to a *kli shelishi*).

169. May one put a *davar gush* on a wet rinsed plate?

A rinsed plate should be wiped dry before putting a *davar gush* on it since cold water should not be in contact with a *kli rishon*. Similarly, the cutlery that one uses to serve or eat the *davar gush* should not be wet. See also Question 173.

170. May one put mayonnaise on a *davar gush*?

This should be avoided since mayonnaise contains raw eggs. This includes manufactured mayonnaise (compare Question 139).

171. May one put butter on a *davar gush*?

Opinions differ about this. Although butter is made from pasteurized milk, some opinions consider the butter to be a raw food.

172. May one put ketchup on a *davar gush*?

Yes. Ketchup is a cooked liquid, and this lenient factor allows the issue of a *davar gush* to be ignored.

173. May one put a *davar gush* onto a plate that is wet from a cooked liquid?

Yes. Since the liquid is cooked, one may be lenient to ignore the issue of *davar gush*. For example, if one has eaten a portion of cholent and there is cold gravy on the plate, he may put a hot piece of meat from the pot onto the plate.

174. May one put a cooked food next to a *davar gush*?

This is permitted whether the cooked food is boiled or baked. Technically, a *davar gush* does *afiya* to what it touches rather than bishul since it is a solid food. Therefore, it cannot affect a baked food because *ein afiya achar afiya*; and even a boiled food is not affected since the *davar gush* is incapable of imparting a roasted taste to it (compare Question 37). For example, one may put a slice of cold meat, whether boiled or roasted, next to hot kugel or cholent.

175. May one put raw vegetables next to a *davar gush*?

• According to many opinions, this should be avoided since the *davar gush* might begin to cook the vegetables or their juice.

• According to some opinions, this is permitted since one does not intend to cook the vegetables and they are not improved by any heat that they receive. Nevertheless, one should not deliberately mix the foods together.

For example: coleslaw with cholent; lettuce with hot fish; pickles with kugel.

It is therefore preferable to serve such foods at separate courses or at least on separate plates.

176. May one serve a *davar gush* on a plate that was used for raw salad?

If the plate is wet from juice of the salad, one should preferably wipe the plate dry before serving the *davar gush* on it (compare Question 169).

177. May one serve hot cake with ice cream?

It is preferable not to do so since ice cream contains raw eggs (compare Question 139). One may be lenient if he is certain that the layer of ice cream touching the hot cake will not reach *yad soledes bo*. This is likely if the ice cream is very cold or the cake is not very hot.

178. May one cut ice cream with a hot knife or spoon?

Yes. However, the knife or spoon should not be heated on a fire or in a *kli rishon*, but it may be heated in a *kli sheini* such as a cup of hot water.

179. May one cool a hot egg from a *kli rishon* in a cup of cold water?

Yes, provided there is sufficient water that it will not reach *yad soledes bo*.

180. May one rinse a hot egg under cold running water?

Yes, since the water will not reach *yad soledes bo*.

Summary - Foods

	Raw; not fully cooked	Baked; roasted	Cooked powders	Boiled
In *kli rishon* off fire; *iruy kli rishon*	✗	✗	✗	✓
In *kli sheini* *yad nichveis*	✗	✗	✓	✓
On a *davar gush*	✗	✓	✓	✓
In a *kli sheini*	✗	✗	✓	✓
In a *kli sheini* via a ladle	✗	✓	✓	✓
In a *kli shelishi*	✓	✓	✓	✓
Examples	Vegetables, spices, lemon, tea[1], cocoa, artificial sweeteners	Roast meat, bread, cookies, Turkish coffee[2], potato kugel	Sugar, instant coffee[3], instant tea, cooked salt	Boiled chicken, meat, noodles

[1] Forbidden in *kli shelishi*.

[2] Forbidden in *kli shelishi* according to some opinions.

[3] Preferably not in *kli sheini* according to some opinions.

Summary - Liquids

	Raw; not fully boiled, except water and oil	Raw; not fully boiled water, oil	Boiled, now cold	Boiled, still warm
In *kli rishon* off fire; *iruy kli rishon*	✗	✗	✗	✓
In *kli sheini yad nichveis*	✗	✗	✓	✓
On a *davar gush*	✗	✗	✓	✓
In a *kli sheini*	✗	✓	✓	✓
In a *kli sheini* via a ladle	✓	✓	✓	✓
In a *kli shelishi*	✓	✓	✓	✓
Examples	Fresh fruit juice	Water, ice, rinsed noodles	Milk, ketchup, cold soup, cold tea essence, manufactured drinks	Warm soup, warm tea essence

Chapter Nine

Shehiya

181. What is meant by *shehiya*?

Literally this means waiting. It refers to placing food on a fire before the commencement of Shabbos so that one will have hot cooked food for the Shabbos meals.

182. What is the basic law of *shehiya*?

According to Torah law, there are absolutely no restrictions of *shehiya*. Theoretically, one could put a raw food on an open fire close to Shabbos and allow it to cook completely on Shabbos. The Torah permits this since the person's action is done before Shabbos, and the food becomes cooked on its own accord. However, *Chazal* forbade this because it could lead to a serious Torah transgression. Since the food is raw when Shabbos begins, the person will be concerned about its progress and may become upset that it is cooking too slowly. In a moment of forgetfulness, he might increase the flame to speed up the cooking and thereby transgress two Torah *melachos* - bishul and *mav'ir* (making a fire). See also Question 358.

183. Is there a permitted way to leave raw food on a fire?

Yes. *Chazal* allow one to place raw food on a fire just before Shabbos on condition that the fire is covered. This is achieved with a gas stove or electric cooker by the use of a blech (Yiddish, meaning a sheet of metal).

184. How does the blech prevent raising the flame?

The blech serves two purposes:

- It reduces the power of the fire. Since this has the opposite effect of the person's desire to hasten the cooking, he will take his mind off the food and not worry about its progress.
- It acts as a reminder. Since one does not usually cook on a covered fire, he will be reminded that is it Shabbos and must not interfere with the flame.

185. Should the blech be placed before or after lighting the fire?

According to some opinions, it should be placed after lighting the fire. Furthermore, it is preferable not to adjust the flame after the blech has been placed.

186. Should the control knobs be covered?

Strictly speaking this is not required, but it is preferable to cover the knobs. This acts as another reminder not to touch the controls and adjust the flame. For this reason, today's standard blech is made with a bent section to cover the control knobs.

187. What if one has only a flat blech?

He should preferably cover the controls with tape or foil, or remove the knobs.

188. What if one has no blech?

He may use anything that will withstand the heat of the flame such as a thick piece of foil.

189. Must the entire stove top be covered?

No, only the flame needs to be covered entirely.

190. What if there is a crack in the blech?

The blech may be used even if the fire can be seen though the crack.

191. Is it sufficient to cover just the control knobs?

No. Although it is not essential to cover the knobs, it is essential to cover the fire.

192. What if the flame is on the highest?

A blech is still required. Although in this situation it is impossible to raise the flame, *Chazal* standardized their decree to cover all cases.

193. Is a blech required for cold water?

Yes. One must not put a kettle of cold water on a fire just before Shabbos unless the fire is covered (see also Question 24). Although water can be drunk cold, there is still concern that one might raise the flame to make the water boil faster.

194. Is a blech required for cold soup?

No, since the soup is a cooked food. Although people prefer soup to be hot rather than cold, a blech is not required for any food or liquid that is fully cooked.

195. Is a blech required for food that is partially cooked?

Strictly speaking, a blech is not required if the food is fit to eat in an emergency. Although there might be a temptation to raise the flame and hasten the cooking, this is minimal since the food is already partially cooked and will probably be ready by the time the meal starts. Nevertheless, it is preferable to use a blech for such food as a safeguard against an inadvertent mistake. In addition, it is sometimes difficult to know when a food is considered edible in an emergency.

196. By which time must the food be partially cooked if no blech is used?

The food must be edible in an emergency by sunset. The following rule is a simple memory aid: The laws of *shehiya* start at *shekiya*. See also Questions 358 and 359.

197. What if the family accepts Shabbos early?

The critical time is still sunset. However, if the entire community accepts Shabbos early, the food should be partially cooked by that time.

198. Is a blech required for water that is partially boiled?

Theoretically, it is permitted to leave cold water on an open flame if it will become *yad soledes bo* by sunset. As explained in Question 14 there is uncertainty about the exact temperature, and in this situation one must be stringent to use the highest figure, i.e. 71°C (160°F). However, this is very impractical for two reasons:

- It is difficult to estimate temperatures.
- If one needs to lift the kettle to take water, he must not return it to the fire unless the water is fully boiled and there is a blech (see next chapter).

Even if the water is boiled in an urn with a spout, one must be very careful not to take any water before it has boiled fully (see Question 43). It is therefore recommended to boil the water fully before Shabbos and leave it on a blech.

199. Is it preferable to always use a blech?

It is perfectly acceptable to leave fully cooked food and fully boiled liquids on a flame without a blech. Nevertheless, it is praiseworthy to use a blech always for the following reasons:

- The food might not be fully cooked when one believes that it is.
- One might wish to remove the pot and return it, in which case a blech is essential (see next chapter).
- One might accidentally lower the flame to prevent the food from burning.

200. Is it preferable not to put raw food on a blech close to Shabbos?

It is perfectly acceptable to put raw food on a blech close to Shabbos. Nevertheless, it is praiseworthy to avoid doing so unless last minute cooking is needed unexpectedly. Since the food is raw at the onset of Shabbos, one might be tempted to do something to hasten the cooking. The blech is a safeguard only against increasing the fire, but there still remains the danger of moving the pot closer to the flame, covering the pot, or stirring the food. All these are Torah transgressions (see Question 43), and therefore it is recommended to ensure that all foods are fully cooked even when using a blech.

Summary

Permitted *Shehiya*	Without a blech	With a blech
Basic law	Partially cooked	Raw
Preferable	Fully cooked	Raw
Praiseworthy	-	Fully cooked

Ovens

201. How do these laws apply to an oven?

If the oven is switched off before sunset, one may leave inside it any type of food whether fully cooked or not. Since there is no fire, the laws of *shehiya* do not apply. *Chazal* were concerned that a person might increase an existing fire but not that he would light a new one. Nevertheless, it is praiseworthy to ensure that the food is fully cooked in order to avoid the mistake of opening and reclosing the door on not fully cooked food while the oven is *yad soledes bo* (see Questions 49 and 50). This applies to both an electric and a gas oven.

202. What if the oven is on at sunset?

The oven, whether electric or gas, is equivalent to a fire without a blech. Even if the heating elements of an electric oven are concealed by the walls and the floor, this is not considered as a covering over the fire. The reason is because the oven is always used like this, and one has done nothing to reduce the fire and act as a reminder that it is Shabbos. Therefore, food left in a lit oven must be at least partially cooked and preferably fully cooked. See also Question 49.

203. Is it preferable to cover the control knob?

Yes. Although this is not equivalent to making a blech (see Question 191), it is worthwhile doing so in order to act as a reminder not to adjust the temperature of the oven.

204. Is there a way to make a blech for an oven?

• For an electric oven, one could theoretically place in the oven a box insert as some people do for Pesach. However, this is rarely done during the year. Alternatively, one could make the equivalent of a blech by covering with thick foil all the areas where the heating elements are situated. This would permit one to leave in the oven even raw food. However, this is not practical since according to some opinions one must cover the areas after the oven has been switched on and not beforehand (see Question 185). In addition, there is not much to be gained by making such a covering since it is not required as long as the food is partially cooked. This is not difficult to ensure. Regarding such a covering for *chazara*, see Question 258.

• For a gas oven, in which the flames are exposed, there is no practical way to make a blech.

205. What if the oven has a Shabbos mode?

This is irrelevant for the laws of *shehiya*. The Shabbos mode in certain models of electric ovens allows one to open the oven door at any time without having an effect on the electricity.

206. When may one open the door of an electric oven with a regular setting?

If the oven is used with a regular setting, there is a thermostat that controls the supply of electricity according to the temperature selected. According to many opinions, one must not open the door while the electricity is off since the sudden loss of heat will trigger the thermostat to switch on the elements almost immediately. However, one may open the door while the electricity is on. Although this will cause the elements to remain on for longer, no new *melacha* is performed and it is therefore permitted.

Note: Inside some ovens there is a fan that operates when the door is closed but stops when the door is opened. Inside some ovens there is a light bulb that goes on when the door is opened. Such fans and lights must be disconnected before Shabbos unless one makes use of the oven timer or a Shabbos clock.

207. How can one tell when the electricity is on?

Many ovens have a signal light that indicates when the electricity is on. Alternatively, one might be able to see the elements glowing red hot through the glass door. If one is unable to determine when the electricity is on, he should set the oven timer or a plug-in Shabbos clock to switch off the oven shortly before one will need to take out the food.

208. May one close the oven door at any time?

Yes. Although this causes the heating elements to remain on for less time, this is so indirect that it is not considered a forbidden *melacha*.

209. When may one open the door of a gas oven?

In a gas oven the flames are burning constantly, and opening the door is forbidden at any time since this causes the flames to flare up. The simplest solution is to set the oven timer to switch off the gas shortly before one will need to take out the food. There might be other alternatives, but they are beyond the scope of this work.

Hotplates, Crockpots, and Urns

210. What are the laws of *shehiya* for an electric hotplate?

- If there is a control knob with which one can adjust the temperature, the hotplate has the same laws as a gas stove. One can make a blech by using foil to cover the hotplate and preferably also the control knob. See also Question 213.
- If there is no control knob, a blech is not required according to most opinions since there is no possibility of increasing the fire. In other words, a non-adjustable hotplate is equivalent to a fire covered with a blech.

Therefore, any type of food, including raw, may be left on a non-adjustable hotplate or a covered adjustable hotplate. Nevertheless, it is praiseworthy to ensure that all foods are fully cooked before Shabbos (see Question 200).

211. What are the laws of *shehiya* for a crockpot?

The same as for a hotplate. Since a standard crockpot has a temperature control knob, it is forbidden to fill the crockpot with raw food and switch it on close to Shabbos unless a blech is made. A blech is not required if the food is partially or fully cooked by sunset, but it is praiseworthy to make one always.

212. How can one make a blech for a crockpot?

The inside of the outer electric pot should be lined with foil. If the heating element is inside the base of the pot, it is sufficient to line just the base. If the heating element is also inside the walls of the pot, one must line the entire inside surface of the pot. In either case, it is preferable also to cover the control knob or remove it.

213. Must the foil be a certain thickness?

Opinions differ whether one may use regular thin foil. It is therefore preferable to use a thick type or to fold thin foil into several layers.

214. What are the laws of *shehiya* for an electric urn?

- If the urn has a control knob that either regulates the time taken to boil or varies the maximum temperature of the water, it is comparable to a fire without a blech. Since there is no way to make a blech for an urn, the water must be at least 71°C (160°F) before sunset and preferably fully boiled. It is also preferable to cover the control knob.

• If the urn has no such control knob, it is comparable to a fire with a blech according to most opinions. Therefore, the water may be cold at the onset of Shabbos, although it is preferable to boil it fully beforehand.

In any event, it is forbidden to take out any water on Shabbos before it has boiled fully (see Question 44).

215. May one take water on Shabbos any time after it has boiled?

In certain types of urns, taking water might involve a problem of *mav'ir*. Some urns are equipped with a thermostat that controls the temperature of the water comparable to an oven that is used on a regular setting (see Question 206). When hot water is removed from the urn, cool air takes its place and this might trigger the heating element to switch on if it was off at the time. Therefore, one should take water only when the element is presently on. This can be verified by a signal light that the urn may have or by listening to the heating element that can be heard easily when it is on.

216. Why do some urns have a *hechsher* for Shabbos?

The water in such urns is kept simmering by a different system in which the heating element goes on and off at regular intervals. Since the temperature of the water has no bearing on this mechanism, one may take water from the urn at any time once it has boiled fully.

217. What if an urn has a water-level indicator?

Some urns are equipped with an external tube that shows the level of the water. This creates a problem that the water in the tube does not boil fully since it is too far from the heating element. When hot water is taken from the urn, some water from the tube enters the urn and becomes fully boiled. There are three practical solutions to this problem:

- Remove the tube and seal the hole where it was attached.
- Seal the top of the tube. This prevents water entering the tube when the urn is filled.
- Do not boil cold water in the urn but rather fill it with water that is boiled in an electric kettle. Although such water cools slightly when entering the tube, it remains sufficiently hot that no bishul will occur when it re-enters the urn.

218. May one use all the water in an electric urn?

No. When the level of water is so low that it does not pour out through the spout, it is forbidden to take out water by tilting the urn. First, the urn is *muktzeh* and must not be moved or tilted. In addition, there is a concern that one might be tempted to add water to the urn to prevent damage to the heating element.

219. What if the urn has a device that turns off the element when the water level is low?

One must stop taking water when the level is close to the point where this device is activated.

220. May central heating be switched on close to Shabbos?

Yes. Although the water in the radiators is cold and there is a thermostatic control that can be adjusted to raise the temperature, nevertheless the restrictions of *shehiya* do not apply. *Chazal* felt that they could trust people to remember not to increase a fire made for the purpose of heating as opposed to one lit for cooking.

221. May one turn on an extra radiator?

No. It is forbidden to open a radiator tap on Shabbos since this causes the cold water in the radiator to mix with the hot water in the pipes, which is the *melacha* of bishul. Even if the radiator was on earlier and the water inside is still warm, one may not turn it on again due to the laws of *chazara* (see next chapter). This is because the water in the radiator will be returned to the boiler which is a fire without a blech.

222. May one turn a radiator off?

Yes, since this is simply allowing a collection of hot water to cool down. It is preferable to do this during a period when the boiler is off. If the boiler is on when the radiator is closed, this causes the boiler to switch off earlier since there is less water in the system to be heated. This should be avoided if possible.

Chapter Ten

Chazara

223. What is meant by *chazara*?

Literally this means returning. It refers to returning food to a fire on Shabbos soon after it was removed from there. *Chazal* restricted this activity and permitted it only when certain conditions are fulfilled.

224. Why is *chazara* restricted?

The basis for this restriction is a concept called *nireh kimevasheil* - resembles cooking. According to the Torah, cold fully cooked food may be placed on a fire on Shabbos to heat up because *ein bishul achar bishul* (see Question 16). However, *Chazal* forbade this since it looks so much like an act of cooking that it might lead one to do actual cooking. Later in this chapter we will discuss permitted ways of reheating cooked food. See also Question 274.

225. How does this restriction apply to *chazara*?

Returning food to a fire also resembles cooking. The mere act of placing a pot of food onto a fire looks like cooking whether the food is cold or it is hot because it was previously on the fire. In order to allow *chazara*, one must satisfy several conditions whose purpose is to remove the appearance of cooking.

226. What are the conditions of *chazara*?

There is a basic pre-condition that the food or liquid must be fully cooked. This is actually not a Rabbinic condition of *chazara* but rather a Torah requirement. If food or liquid is removed from a fire before it is fully cooked, it is a *melacha* of bishul to return it (see Questions 15 and 24). Aside from this pre-condition there are four Rabbinic conditions of *chazara*:

1. The fire must have a blech.
2. The food must be removed with the intention to return it.
3. The food must be held the entire time.
4. The food must be still warm when returned.

According to some opinions, there is a fifth condition: the food must not be transferred to a *kli sheini* before returning it. Details of these conditions will be discussed shortly.

Note: *Sephardim* have more lenient rules for *chazara*.

227. How do these conditions remove the appearance of cooking?

• The purpose of the blech is to make the fire an unusual place to cook on. Placing food on such a fire does not look very much like cooking since one usually cooks on an open flame.

• The other three conditions create a connection between the time the food was on the fire before it was removed and the time that it was returned. This form of *chazara* does not look like a new act of cooking, but rather it is considered as a continuation of the food's previous position on the fire.

228. Why is a person's intention relevant?

The concern of *nireh kimevasheil* is not the same as the more general decree of *maris ayin*. In cases that involve *maris ayin* a person's intention is irrelevant because the problem lies in giving a wrong impression to onlookers. In contrast, *nireh kimevasheil* is for the person himself. One must not do an act that resembles cooking in case this leads him to do actual cooking. When he has the correct intention, he knows that he is only returning food and not starting a new act of cooking.

229. What is the meaning of the fifth condition?

According to some opinions, if the food is put into a *kli sheini* it becomes totally disconnected from the fire, and returning it is considered to be a new act that resembles cooking. See Questions 242-244 for further details.

230. May a pot be returned to a different fire?

Yes, provided the second fire has a blech. One may even transfer a pot from an open fire to a covered fire since a blech is required only at the place of returning and not at the place of removing. For example, one may take a pot out of the oven and place it on the blech on the stove whether or not he removes some food. Although the oven has no blech (see Question 202), this is permitted since the stove has a blech. See also Question 262.

231. May one cover a fire with a blech on Shabbos?

Yes. A blech is not *muktzeh*, and it may be placed over a fire on Shabbos. Care is needed on two accounts:

• If the blech is to cover a gas flame (as opposed to an electric burner), it must be placed gently so as not to put out the fire. The fact that the flame spreads out is of no concern.

• The blech must be sufficiently thick that it will not become red hot (see Question 2).

232. May a pot on an open fire be returned there after placing a blech?

Yes. It sometimes happens that a fully cooked pot of food is left on an open fire (see Question 199) because one was not planning to do *chazara*. If on Shabbos one decides to do *chazara*, he may lift the pot, put a blech on the fire, and return the pot. The same applies if he realizes that the food might burn without a blech.

233. What exactly is meant by intending to return the food?

The person who takes the food from the fire should have in mind that he is removing it only temporarily and wishes to return it shortly. If he removes it with the intention of keeping it off the fire and then changes his mind, he has not fulfilled this condition (see Question 248).

234. What if he has no particular intention?

According to many opinions, it is considered as though he fulfilled the condition because he did not specifically intend to keep it off the fire.

235. What if he intended to return it but did not do so?

Nothing wrong was done. One may always have the intention to return a pot just in case this is necessary even if in the end he decides to keep it off the fire.

236. What is meant by holding the pot the entire time?

• According to most opinions, this means that it is sufficient to keep one's hand around a handle of the pot even if the pot is put down completely.

• According to other opinions, one must be supporting the pot at least partially. This can be achieved in any of the following ways:

> • Hold the pot in mid-air.
> • Rest less than half of the base on the edge of a table or counter.
> • Rest one point of the base on a table or counter and raise the other side of the pot slightly.

237. May one give the pot to someone else to hold?

Yes.

238. Who should return the pot?

The person who removed it from the fire.

239. Must the pot cover also be held?

No.

240. How warm must the food be when it is returned?

Warm enough to be enjoyed if someone wants hot food (see Question 26).

241. Does this condition apply to all types of foods?

• Regarding a liquid or a mixture of food and liquid, all opinions agree that it must be warm when returned. To return a cold liquid to a fire not only resembles cooking, but it is also actual cooking because of the rule *yeish bishul achar bishul* (see Question 25).

• Regarding a dry food, most opinions permit returning it even if it went cold in the meantime. Of course, this is provided the other conditions are fulfilled. E.g. a pan of kugel.

242. When is the fifth condition relevant?

As mentioned above, some opinions forbid *chazara* to food in a *kli sheini* (see Question 229). This is relevant when a pot of food on the fire such as cholent is drying out and one wishes to add hot water to it from an urn. To do this by using a cup is subject to dispute since the cup of water is a *kli sheini*.

243. What is the final ruling?

It is preferable to use another method if possible.

244. Which other methods are available?

• The pot of cholent can be removed from the fire and held under the faucet of the urn while water is added directly. The cholent may then be returned to the fire provided there is a blech. Care should be taken to avoid meaty steam reaching the urn.

• A ladle or cup can be used to scoop out water from the top of the urn. Such water is considered to be *kli rishon* and may be added to the cholent (see Question 156). The pot of cholent should preferably be moved off the fire while adding the water since there will be some turbulence to the food which is comparable to stirring (see Question 54). If the cholent cannot be moved, the water should be poured in gently to minimize the turbulence.

245. What if the cholent is hotter than the water in the urn?

In some types of electric urns the water does not reach boiling point (100°C, 212°F). If the temperature of the cholent is higher than that of the water, transferring the water would be a forbidden act of cooking (see Question 24). The solution is to prepare a pot of boiled water before Shabbos and leave it on the blech. This may be added to the cholent when necessary even if the water is not as hot as the cholent since it was boiled (see Question 25). The cholent should preferably be moved off the fire while adding the water.

246. May one add cold cooked food to a pot that is being returned to the blech?

No. Before returning a pot of food to the blech it is forbidden to add any food that was not previously on the fire. This certainly looks as though one is cooking the added food. It goes without saying that one must not add food, even if fully cooked, into a pot on the blech (see Question 274).

Mistakes

247. Is *chazara* permitted if not all the conditions were fulfilled?

• A blech is essential and *chazara* is never permitted without it.

• If a liquid went cold, it must not be returned to the blech.

• If a dry food went cold, it may be returned to the blech.

• If food or liquid was put into a *kli sheini*, it may be returned to the blech.

• Regarding intention and holding, see the following questions.

248. What if one intended to keep the food off the fire?

If there is a reasonable need for the food to be returned to the blech, one may do so provided he is still holding it.

249. What if one put the pot down and removed his hand?

If there is a reasonable need for the food to be returned to the blech, one may do so provided he had intention to return it. He should resume holding the pot as soon as he realizes that he let go of it. However, if the pot was placed on the floor or put into the refrigerator, one may not return it even if he had intention to do so since this is considered a new placement.

250. What if one intended to keep the food off and removed his hand?

Since he is missing both of these conditions, he may not return the food in most circumstances. However, if the food is essential for one of the meals and it would be very difficult to manage without it, one may return it. Even in this case, it is preferable not to put it directly on the blech but rather above another pot or on an inverted empty pan (see Questions 275 and 280).

251. What if one removed the wrong pot and intended to keep it off?

If he did not realize until he let go of the pot, opinions differ whether he may return it to the blech. Therefore:

- If the food is not essential, he should preferably not return it.
- If the food is essential, he may return it. Nevertheless, it is preferable to place it above another pot on the blech or on an inverted empty pan if possible.

252. What if the fire under the blech blew out accidentally?

• If the food is still warm, it may be moved to a different covered fire. Since one did not physically remove the food from the fire and he wished the food to remain on the fire, he may move it to another fire.

• If the food went cold, it may not be transferred to another fire. This applies even to a dry food since it is a new placement (contrast Question 241).

253. May one turn off the gas?

Yes, but preferably in an unusual way since the knob is *muktzeh*. For example, one may turn it with one's elbow. This is permitted even if automatic sparking will occur as one turns off the gas.

254. What if the electricity shut off?

If cooked foods were left on an electric appliance such as a cooker, hotplate, or crockpot, and the electric supply was disconnected, one may move the foods to a different covered fire provided they are still warm.

255. May one leave the food there until the electricity is reconnected?

• One may do so if the electricity is connected in a permitted way. For example, by Jews in a life-threatening situation or by gentiles in a city in *Chutz La'aretz*.

• One may not do so if the electricity is connected in a forbidden way. For example, by Jews where there is no danger to life or by a gentile for a private individual.

These rules apply whether the food remains warm or goes cold in the meantime.

Note: There might be a health hazard in eating such food that was not kept hot continuously.

256. What if hot food was left on a hotplate that was accidentally not switched on before Shabbos?

One may move the food on Shabbos to a covered fire provided the food is fully cooked and still warm.

Ovens

257. May food be returned to a hot oven that has switched off?

The laws of *chazara* do not apply since an oven is not used when off and placing food there does not resemble cooking. However, actual bishul could occur since the oven is still hot. Therefore, one may put there only the following:

- Cooked foods, whether hot or cold. For example: meat, chicken, vegetables, kugel, and challah.
- Cooked liquids that were hot and are still warm. For example, a pot of soup.

Such items may be placed inside the oven even if one had no previous intention to do so, and one was not holding it.

258. May food be returned to an oven that is on?

No. Even if one covers the heating elements as explained for the purpose of *shehiya* (Question 204), this is not sufficient for *chazara*. Theoretically, *chazara* would be permitted if one placed in the oven a box insert as some people do for Pesach. However, this is rarely done during the year.

259. What if one compartment is on and the other is off?

One may put food inside the compartment that is off according to the restrictions explained in Question 257. If that compartment is not very hot and cold food would never reach *yad soledes bo*, one may put there any type of food or liquid including cold and raw.

260. May one put food into a warming drawer?

The rules of the previous question apply. Although the drawer is switched on, it is not a place used for cooking and the laws of *chazara* are not applicable. One must only avoid actual bishul.

261. May one transfer food to the blech from an oven that a timer switched off?

If the timer was set correctly and the oven switched off as planned, one may not transfer the food to the blech. Once the oven has switched off, it is as though one removed the food without intending to return it and is no longer holding it (see Question 250).

262. What if one needs the food to stay hot for longer?

He should transfer it to the blech (or hotplate) before the oven switches off. If he is unable to open the oven door because the elements are off temporarily (see Question 206) and the oven is due to switch off shortly, he should have the intention to transfer the food as soon as the oven switches off. He may then transfer the food after the oven switches off.

263. What if the timer was set incorrectly and switched the oven off too early?

The food may be transferred to the blech (or hotplate) provided the food is still warm (compare Question 252).

264. What if the food in the oven is needed at two different times?

An example of such a situation is when young children need to eat the evening meal before the rest of the family. Since it is forbidden to return food to an oven that is on, some other method must be used. Ideally, each food should be divided into two pots before Shabbos, one for the children and the other for the rest of the family. If the situation arose unexpectedly, the food may be removed from the oven, served to the children, and then placed on a blech or hotplate. The conditions of *chazara* must be fulfilled (see Question 230).

265. What if there is nowhere else to return the food?

In times of need, one may remove some food from the pots while they are inside the oven. Although this is usually forbidden (see Question 54), it is permitted in this situation where there is no way to do *chazara* and the food is needed urgently. One may use this method only in an unexpected situation, but one may not plan from *erev Shabbos* to serve food like this.

266. May the pot or oven rack be pulled out slightly?

Yes, one may do this to facilitate the removal of food. The pot or rack may be pushed back inside the oven provided the pot was not taken completely out of the oven.

Hotplates, Crockpots, and Urns

267. What are the laws of *chazara* for a hotplate with controls?

Since such a hotplate is used for cooking, it has the same laws as a gas stove. It must be covered with foil to act as a blech, and all the other conditions must be fulfilled. Preferably, the controls should also be covered. See also Question 213.

268. What are the laws for a hotplate without controls?

There are various opinions regarding *chazara*:

• According to *Sephardic* opinions, the laws of *chazara* do not apply at all. Since such a hotplate is rarely used for cooking, placing food on it does not look like cooking. Therefore, it is comparable to a warming drawer where any cooked food may be put (see Question 260).

• According to most *Ashkenazic* opinions, a covering of foil is not required but all the other conditions of *chazara* must be fulfilled. Since it is possible, although unusual, to cook on such a hotplate, it is comparable to a fire that is covered with a blech. Therefore, one may not put food onto it unless the food was previously on a fire and was removed temporarily.

• According to some *Ashkenazic* opinions, all the rules of *chazara* apply including the need to cover the hotplate with foil. This is because *Chazal* standardized their rules for all cases (compare Question 192).

269. What are the laws for a crockpot?

All the conditions of *chazara* must be fulfilled. The inside of the outer electric pot must be lined with foil as for *shehiya* (see Question 212).

270. What are the laws for an electric urn?

It is forbidden to return water to an electric urn. This is because it is impossible to make a blech for it, and this is as essential requirement for *chazara* to an appliance used for cooking.

271. May one use a Shabbos clock to switch on an oven, hotplate, or crockpot?

• On Shabbos it is forbidden to place any type of food into an oven or crockpot or onto a hotplate that is set to come on with a Shabbos clock. Even if one does so while the electricity is off, this is considered as placement on a fire and resembles cooking.

• Opinions differ whether food may be placed on a hotplate or in a crockpot on *erev Shabbos* when the appliance is off, and it is set to come on during Shabbos. According to the opinions who permit it, the appliance must be covered with foil to act as a blech but the food can even be raw. This arrangement is not possible for an oven since making a blech is not practical (see Question 204).

272. May one use a Shabbos clock to switch on an electric urn?

No, since it is impossible to make a blech for an urn. Therefore, it is forbidden to fill an urn with cold water on *erev Shabbos* and set a Shabbos clock to boil it on Shabbos.

273. May one use a Shabbos clock to switch off a cooking appliance?

Yes. One may set a Shabbos clock on an oven, hotplate, crockpot, or urn to switch off during Shabbos after one has finished using it. It is forbidden to reuse it if it switches on again towards the end of Shabbos.

Reheating Cooked Foods

274. How may one reheat a cold cooked food?

As explained earlier, *Chazal* forbid reheating cooked food in a way that resembles cooking. It is therefore forbidden to place food such as chicken, kugel, or challah in any of the following places:

- On a blech that is covering a gas or electric stove (see also Question 289).
- On a hotplate with controls (see also Question 268).
- In an oven that is on.
- Inside a pot that is in any of the above places.
- Inside a crockpot.

One may only reheat such food in a way that does not resemble cooking.

275. Which ways do not resemble cooking?

One may reheat cooked food in any of the following places:

- In an oven that is off but hot.
- On a hot radiator or heater.
- On top of a crockpot or urn.
- On top of a pot of food that is on a blech or a hotplate.
- On a counter near the stove.

This is permitted even if the food will reach *yad soledes bo*.

Note: If the cooked food is wet or is covered with congealed fat, see Questions 83-85.

276. May one place the food on a pot that is on an uncovered fire?

Yes. For example: a pot on a hotplate with controls that is not covered with foil, a crockpot that is not lined with foil, or an urn. Although there is no blech, one may reheat cooked food on top of such pots.

277. May one reheat food in a double boiler?

A double boiler is a set of two pots that are placed one on top of the other. The base of the upper pot serves as the cover for the lower pot, and different foods are cooked in the two pots at the same time. Since this is a normal way of cooking, it is forbidden to reheat cooked food inside the upper pot whether the upper pot is empty or already contains food.

278. May one place food on the upturned cover of a pot on the fire?

Yes, since this is not a normal way to cook food. It is permitted even if the upturned cover dips into the pot and the food is within the walls of the pot.

279. May one place food in an empty pan on the blech?

If the base of the pan is on the blech, it is considered as merely another blech. The fact that there are two blechs does not remove the appearance of cooking, and therefore it is forbidden to place food in the pan.

280. May one place food on an upturned pan on the blech?

- According to many opinions, this is permitted since it is not a usual way to cook.
- According to other opinions, this is forbidden since the pan is still considered as a second blech, and one may not put food on a blech.

281. Must the pan have a minimum depth?

No. According to the opinion that allows an upturned pan, one may use even a shallow pan if there is a noticeable air space between the food and the blech.

282. Must the pan be on the blech before Shabbos?

No, it may be put there on Shabbos. However, due to the laws of *muktzeh*, it is better to use a heat resistant bowl or plate. Alternatively, one may designate before Shabbos a specific pan for this purpose. If nothing else is available, one may use a regular pan.

283. May one use an upturned pan on a hotplate?

- If the hotplate has no controls, one may use an upturned pan according to many opinions. Compare Question 280.
- If the hotplate has controls, one may only use an upturned pan if the hotplate is covered with foil to act as a blech. Otherwise, the pan is considered as the blech and a second upturned pan is required on top of the first one. See Question 267.

Areas of the Blech

284. Do all areas of the blech have the same rules for *chazara*?

No. The blech is divided into three areas:

1. Directly over the fire.

2. Not over the fire but hot enough for cold food to reach *yad soledes bo* if placed there.

3. Far from the fire and not hot enough for cold food to reach *yad soledes bo* if placed there.

285. What are the rules for these areas?

As explained earlier, it is forbidden to stir or remove food from a pot on area 1 but permitted on area 2 (see Question 53). However, regarding *chazara* these two areas have identical rules as follows:

• A pot may be moved back and forth between areas 1 and 2. One does not need to hold the pot or have intention to return it. Therefore, if one wishes to remove food from a pot on area 1, he may move it to area 2, take the food, and return the pot to area 1. Of course, the food must be fully cooked.

• Nothing may be placed on area 1 or 2 unless it was previously on a fire and the conditions of *chazara* were fulfilled. For example, one may not heat a challah or kugel by putting it on either area.

286. May food on top of a pot on the blech be moved down to these areas?

No. When food is placed on a pot on the blech, it is considered to be near the fire but not on it. Even if it was there from before Shabbos, it may not be moved down to area 1 or 2 since this appears to be an act of cooking. If the lower pot is needed first, one should transfer the food on it onto another pot. According to many opinions, one may put it on an upturned pan.

287. May food on an upturned pan be moved down to these areas?

According to most opinions, food that was left on an upturned pan from before Shabbos is considered near the fire but not on it. Therefore, it may not be moved down to area 1 or 2.

288. What if food was moved from the blech to an upturned pan on Shabbos?

If it was moved there with the intention of returning it later to the blech, it may be moved down to area 1 or 2 if there is a reasonable need to do so. However, one may not plan to do this since the food is being removed from the fire and is not being held the entire time (see Question 249).

289. What are the rules for the third area?

According to most opinions, area 3 is considered to be near the fire but not on it. Therefore:

• Any type of food or liquid, whether cooked or raw, may be put on this area. There is no restriction of bishul since nothing will reach *yad soledes bo*, and there is no resemblance of cooking since it is impossible to cook anything there.

• Any type of food or liquid that was put on this area before Shabbos may not be moved from there on Shabbos to area 1 or 2 since this resembles cooking.

290. May food on top of a pot on the blech be moved down to area 3?

Yes. Since both positions are considered to be near the fire but not on it, one may move food from on top of a pot on the blech to area 3. The reverse is permitted for cooked foods. However, raw foods and cold liquids must not be transferred from area 3 to on top of a pot on the blech since they might begin to cook there.

291. May food on an upturned pan be moved down to this area?

Yes, and according to most opinions the reverse is also permitted for cooked foods.

292. May food be moved from area 1 to area 3 and back again?

Ideally, this should not be done since food should not be moved from area 3 to area 1. However, if food was moved from area 1 to area 3 and the person who moved it intended to return it, he may move it back to area 1. Therefore, if one wishes to move food from area 1 in order to serve it or to prevent it from burning, he should take care to move it only to area 2 and not to area 3. Similarly, food should not be moved from area 2 to area 3 with the plan to return it. If this happened, and the one who moved it intended to return it, he may move it back to area 2 and even to area 1.

293. What are the laws of a pot that is partially on area 2 and partially on area 3?

It is considered as though it is totally on area 2. Therefore, a pot that was left in this position from before Shabbos may be moved to area 1 or 2 on Shabbos.

Summary for moving cooked foods

	To area 1	To area 2	To area 3
From area 1	-	Yes	Yes
From area 2	Yes	-	Yes
From area 3	No[1]	No[1]	-
From upturned pan	No	No	Yes
From on top of a pot	No	No	Yes
From fridge	No	No	Yes[2]

[1] See Question 292.

[2] Permitted even for raw foods and cold liquids.

Chapter Eleven

Hatmana

294. What is meant by *hatmana*?

Literally this means concealing. It refers to the insulation of a pot of hot food by wrapping it with various materials. *Chazal* made limitations to this activity out of concern that it might lead to transgressions of bishul or *mav'ir*. Compare Question 182.

295. Which materials are included?

All materials are included, but they are divided into two categories with different laws:

• *Mosif hevel*: A type that adds heat to the food. For example: hot ashes, sand, lime, wet grass, electric blanket.

• *Ma'amid hevel*: A type that maintains the food's heat. For example: towels, foil, plastic, paper.

296. What if the pot of food is on a fire?

When a pot of food is on any source of heat, all materials that wrap it are considered as *mosif hevel*. This is because the combination of heat and wrapping causes the food to get hotter. This applies to even a relatively weak source of heat such as a radiator. Similarly, it applies to a pot on top of another pot on the blech or on area 3 of the blech.

Note: Certain situations of *hatmana* might present a fire risk. When wrapping pots in a permitted way, great care must be taken to avoid such a hazard.

297. What are the laws for *mosif hevel* materials?

This type of *hatmana* is severely restricted in the following ways:

• It is forbidden whether the pot is wrapped on Shabbos, or it is wrapped before Shabbos and left in that state when Shabbos begins.

• It applies to hot food in any *kli*; whether *rishon*, *sheini*, or *shelishi*.

• It applies even to cold food.

See also Question 305 for permitted methods of *hatmana*.

298. What are the laws for *ma'amid hevel* materials?

• It is forbidden to wrap a *kli rishon* on Shabbos with such material, but one may wrap it before Shabbos and leave it wrapped until it is needed.

• It is permitted to wrap a *kli sheini* or *shelishi* with such material even on Shabbos.

299. What if one accepts Shabbos early?

He may still do *hatmana* with *ma'amid hevel* until sunset or until the entire community accepts Shabbos.

300. What are practical examples of these laws?

- If one puts a pot of food on another pot on the blech, one may not wrap the upper pot with a cloth or towel to keep it warm. This is forbidden even before Shabbos.
- Before Shabbos one may heat up a pot of food, place it on a counter or table, wrap it with a towel or blanket, and leave it like this until needed for the meal. However, if the pot was removed from the blech after sunset, one may not wrap it unless the food is first transferred to a *kli sheini*.

301. May one add material on Shabbos to a previously wrapped pot?

Yes. In the above example when a pot on the table was wrapped fully before Shabbos, one may add another layer of material on Shabbos for extra efficiency. However if the pot was wrapped only partially before Shabbos, one may not wrap it fully on Shabbos.

302. May one exchange the wrapping for a better one?

Yes. Although it is forbidden to wrap a *kli rishon* on Shabbos, changing a wrapping on Shabbos is not a new act of *hatmana* but rather a continuation of what was started before Shabbos. Similarly, one may remove the wrapping in order to serve the food and then rewrap it.

303. Must one have the intention to rewrap it?

No. After serving the food, one may rewrap the pot even if this was not planned.

304. What if the wrapping fell off?

The pot may be rewrapped provided one knows that the wrapping fell off after sunset.

305. Are there permitted ways to do *hatmana*?

There are two general methods:

- To wrap the pot only partially.
- To wrap the pot fully but leave a space between the pot and the wrapping material.

These types of *hatmana* are permitted even on Shabbos and for all materials, including *mosif hevel*.

306. How much wrapping is considered partial?

A substantial amount of the pot must be left unwrapped so that the effectiveness of the wrapping is reduced significantly. For example, one may completely wrap the sides of the pot but leave the pot cover unwrapped. Alternatively, one may place a folded towel over the pot and draped around the sides but leave the lowest inch or two of the sides unwrapped.

307. Isn't the base of the pot unwrapped?

In most cases, the base of the pot is considered to be wrapped by the surface on which it is sitting. For example: a blech, a hotplate, a table, another pot.

308. What if the pot is on a trivet?

A trivet is a stand on which hot pots are placed. If the pot is much wider than the trivet, one may wrap the pot cover and all the sides of the pot since a significant area of the base remains unwrapped. However, the wrapping must not reach the table or surface on which the trivet stands since this would be considered as wrapping completely.

309. May one totally wrap two adjacent pots?

If one encloses two pots with a single wrapping, there will be a large area of each pot unwrapped. However, this should not be done since the pots are insulated very efficiently and it is therefore equivalent to a total wrapping. The same applies to several pots wrapped together.

310. How much space must be left between the pot and the wrapping for this method?

Even a small recognizable space is enough since this reduces the efficiency of the wrapping.

311. Is the space next to the handles sufficient?

No. When a pot is wrapped with a towel, a space is bound to form next to the protruding handles. This does not qualify to permit *hatmana* since one is required to deliberately create a space that he would prefer not to have to leave open.

312. May some of the wrapping material touch the pot?

Yes, on condition that a substantial part of the wrapping does not touch the pot.

313. How should one create a sufficient space?

There are two practical suggestions:

- Replace the pot cover with something wide, such as a board, tray, or larger lid. A towel, blanket, etc. may then be wrapped totally around the pot and its wide cover.
- Place the pot inside a larger pot and wrap the outer pot completely.

314. Is food in an oven subject to the laws of *hatmana*?

No. When a pot of food is left inside an oven, it is not considered as *hatmana*. The hot air that surrounds the pot is not called wrapping material since it is intangible, and the oven is not a wrapper since it does not touch the pot.

315. What if the pot in the oven is fully wrapped?

- If the oven is on, this is forbidden even before Shabbos since it is *hatmana* with *mosif hevel*.
- If the oven is off, it is permitted to leave the pot there before Shabbos, but it is forbidden to place the pot inside the hot oven on Shabbos even if it was wrapped before Shabbos.

316. Does *hatmana* apply to a Thermos?

No. Although the outer cover totally wraps the inner container, it is considered to be one unit. Even if it would be viewed as one item wrapping another, it is a *kli sheini* with *ma'amid hevel* material. This is permitted even on Shabbos (see Question 298).

317. May one wrap a hot water bottle in a towel?

Yes, since it is a *kli sheini* with *ma'amid hevel* material.

318. May one wrap an urn?

It may be wrapped only partially, such as by leaving the lid unwrapped. Since there is a fire under the water, this is a situation of *mosif hevel* for which total *hatmana* is forbidden. This applies to both an electric urn and one that stands on the blech.

319. May one submerge a baby bottle in hot water?

It is permitted provided the top of the bottle is outside the water, which in any case is usually true. The hot water is considered to be *mosif hevel* wrapping material, and therefore submerging totally would be forbidden. See also Questions 111 and 112 regarding bishul.

320. May the baby bottle be wrapped after it has been heated?

Yes, since it is a *kli sheini* with *ma'amid hevel* material.

321. May wrapped food be heated above an urn or pot?

According to most opinions, one may wrap a food such as challah or kugel in a piece of foil or plastic bag and heat it on top of an urn or pot. This is permitted even on Shabbos although it appears to be complete wrapping with *mosif hevel*. The reason is because the wrapping around the food is considered like a container or pot. Just as one may place a pot of food on an urn or pot, one may also put there a wrapped food.

322. May the food be wrapped in two pieces of foil?

If both pieces wrap the food completely, it is forbidden. The inner piece of foil can be considered like a container, but the outer piece is *hatmana*. However, if the outer piece is not for the purpose of heat but it is needed to hold the food together, to keep it fresh, etc., it is permitted. One may also take a large piece of foil, fold it into several layers, and wrap the food once. The multi-layered foil is considered a single thick container.

323. May an aluminum pan of kugel be completely wrapped with foil and heated this way?

Yes. Since the pan has no lid, the piece of foil is considered to be the pan cover, and therefore it is considered as though the top of the pan is not wrapped. Although the sides and base of the pan will be wrapped with a layer of foil, this is considered only partial wrapping.

324. May wrapped food be put inside a pot of cholent before Shabbos?

If one wishes to wrap kishke etc. in foil or a plastic bag and place it inside the cholent, the rules are as follows:

• If the wrapped food is not totally submerged in the cholent, it is permitted. The wrapping is a container, and the hot cholent is an additional wrapping that is only partial.

• If the wrapped food is totally submerged, it is forbidden according to most opinions. This is because the cholent is considered as a total wrapping of *mosif hevel*. However, if the wrapped food is not sealed tightly and the liquid of the cholent seeps into the food, it is permitted since the food is then considered part of the cholent. One could poke holes in the wrapping to guarantee that the liquid seeps through or wrap the food in a cloth bag.

325. May one put eggs into the cholent or soup before Shabbos?

Yes. Since the egg shell is porous and the flavor seeps through, the egg is considered part of the cholent.

326. May one heat a hard-boiled egg in a bowl of hot water on Shabbos?

It is forbidden if the egg is completely submerged in the water. Although the shell is porous there is no transfer of taste, and the egg cannot be considered as part of the water.

327. Does *hatmana* apply to a crockpot?

• According to most opinions, using a crockpot does not involve *hatmana*. Although the inner pot of food is surrounded by the outer electric pot, there is only one cover on top and partial wrapping is permitted even with *mosif hevel*. However, one must not drape a towel over the top since this would create a total wrapping.

• According to some opinions, normal use of a crockpot is forbidden *hatmana* since it is highly efficient despite the single cover. Partial wrapping is permitted only when one deliberately leaves an area uncovered to decrease the effectiveness of the insulation.

328. What can be done to satisfy all opinions?

One should slightly raise the inner pot by placing something inside the outer pot such as an empty can, a few stones, or crushed balls of foil. This has the effect of uncovering the base of the inner pot and the upper rim, which changes the situation to one of partial wrapping.

Note: The can, stones, or balls of foil do not qualify as a blech for *shehiya* and *chazara*. For these activities, a lining of foil is needed (see Questions 212 and 269).

Chapter Twelve

Bathing

329. Are there any restrictions to bathing on Shabbos?

Yes. In the days of old when people bathed in public bathhouses, the attendants would sometimes light fires and heat the water on Shabbos claiming that they prepared it before Shabbos. Therefore, *Chazal* made several restrictions to bathing with hot water even if it was heated before Shabbos. Although today people bathe at home privately, nevertheless the rules still apply since one might forget and heat water on Shabbos for this purpose.

330. What are the restrictions?

There are two basic restrictions:

- One may not wash the majority of the body with hot water even if it was heated before Shabbos.
- One may not wash any part of the body with hot water that was heated on Shabbos even in a permitted way.

Therefore, it is permitted only to wash the minority of the body with hot water that was heated before Shabbos. For example: hands, face, and feet.

Note: Opening the hot water faucet is usually forbidden, see Question 64. Hot water for bathing may be taken from an urn.

331. Do the same rules apply to warm water?

No, warm water has the same rules as cold water (see Question 339). For these laws, warm water means below normal body temperature (37°C; 98.6°F). Contrast Question 14.

332. May hot water be used to wash most of the body one limb at a time?

No. However, if one washed parts of the body and later decided to wash other parts, he may use hot water (heated before Shabbos). This is permitted even if the total area washed is the majority of the body provided that each time only a minority is washed. It is forbidden to plan in advance to wash oneself this way.

333. May one use water that a gentile heated for himself on Shabbos?

No. Such water may not be used for washing any part of the body since it was heated on Shabbos.

334. What if water was heated on Shabbos by itself?

Such water has the rules of water that was heated before Shabbos. For example, an electric urn was switched on close to Shabbos, or a kettle of cold water was placed on a blech close to Shabbos (see Questions 214 and 193). After the water has boiled (see Question 44), one may use it to wash the minority of the body.

Note: Water that is heated by solar panels is considered to be heated by itself, but one may not usually open the hot water faucet (see Question 64).

335. May one mix hot and cold water for bathing?

Yes, one may use such a mixture to wash the minority of the body. Although the cold water becomes heated on Shabbos, this is an incidental side effect, and the main purpose of mixing is to cool down the hot water. See also Questions 110 and 132 regarding how to mix the water.

336. Do the same rules apply for children?

Basically, yes. Therefore, if a baby or young child needs to be bathed on Shabbos, one must avoid washing the majority of his body unless the water is just lukewarm.

337. May a sick person be more lenient?

Yes. If a person is ill or in pain, he may wash even his entire body with hot water that was heated before Shabbos.

338. May one hold one's wet hands near a fire?

If the water will reach body temperature, this is forbidden since it is considered as though one is washing with hot water that was heated on Shabbos. The same applies to putting wet hands near a hot radiator, urn, or hot pot of food. However, one may first warm one's dry hands and then wash them with cold water.

339. May one have a cold shower?

There is a well-established custom dating back hundreds of years not to wash one's entire body with cold water on Shabbos. The reason is because this might lead to squeezing one's wet hair, which is forbidden. However, if one avoids washing the hair, one may shower the rest of the body with cold water.

340. May one shower the entire body with cold water in times of need?

Yes, if he is suffering from the extreme heat. Care should be taken when drying the hair to rub only lightly in order to avoid squeezing.

341. May a man wash his beard?

Yes. He may use either cold water or hot water that was heated before Shabbos.

Mikveh

342. May a woman immerse in a hot *mikveh* on Shabbos?

If possible, she should immerse only in a warm *mikveh* that is below normal body temperature (see Question 331). However, even if the water is hotter than that, she may still immerse. In any event, she should be careful when drying her hair to avoid squeezing.

343. May a man immerse in a hot *mikveh*?

- According to many opinions, it is forbidden.
- According to some opinions, it is permitted provided he immerses and leaves immediately without lingering in the water to enjoy the warmth. He should be careful when drying his hair to avoid squeezing.

344. May a man immerse in a cold *mikveh*?

The widespread custom is to permit immersing in a cold *mikveh* or in a warm mikveh that is below normal body temperature. He should be careful when drying his hair to avoid squeezing.

Chapter Thirteen

Benefitting from Forbidden Cooking

345. May one eat food that was cooked on Shabbos?

This depends on several factors as follows:

- Was the cooking forbidden by the Torah or Rabbinically?
- Was it done deliberately or accidentally?
- Is the food needed urgently?
- Is there an opinion that permits such cooking (see Question 368)?

In certain cases, *Chazal* imposed a penalty forbidding one to eat the food in order not to benefit from the desecration of Shabbos.

346. What is the law for a deliberate Torah transgression?

- The person who cooked the food may never eat it.
- Others may not eat it on Shabbos. They may eat it immediately after Shabbos if this type of transgression does not occur frequently.

347. What if the person openly transgresses Shabbos regularly, *chas veshalom*?

The food may not be eaten by others immediately after Shabbos. They must wait after Shabbos the length of time that it took to cook the food.

348. May the one who cooked the food sell it?

Yes, he may sell it and benefit from the money. Similarly, he may give the food to another person as a gift.

349. What if the Torah transgression was accidental?

• If the raw food was *muktzeh*, it may not be moved and certainly not eaten by anyone on Shabbos. Everyone may eat it immediately after Shabbos, including the one who cooked it. For example: meat, chicken, fish, potatoes.

• If the raw food was not *muktzeh* and it is not needed urgently, it may be eaten only after Shabbos by everyone. For example: apples, carrots.

• If the raw food was not *muktzeh* and it is needed urgently, it may be eaten on Shabbos by everyone.

350. What is meant by needed urgently?

This usually means that there is no other food to eat. If there are visitors, one may be more flexible in deciding whether the food is needed urgently. In any event, a rav should be consulted to assess the situation.

351. What if one forgot the *halacha*?

If one knew that this form of cooking is forbidden but he forgot, it is considered as an accidental transgression. The same applies if he ruled incorrectly and thought it was permitted.

352. What if one followed the ruling of a rav who erred?

It is considered an accidental transgression.

353. What if a child cooked food?

- If he did it for himself, the food may be eaten on Shabbos by everyone.
- If he did it for an adult, the food may not be eaten by anyone until after Shabbos. In addition, one must wait after Shabbos the length of time that it took to cook the food.

There is no difference whether the cooking was done deliberately or accidentally.

354. What is the law for a Rabbinic transgression?

- If the cooking was done deliberately, the food may be eaten immediately after Shabbos by everyone.
- If it was done accidentally, the food may be eaten on Shabbos by everyone.
- The rules are different for *shehiya*, *chazara*, and *hatmana*. See Questions 358, 360, and 364.

355. What if someone added cold water to an urn?

No water may be taken until the added water has boiled fully. After that, one may take hot water until the original quantity of water has been used.

356. What if someone added cold water to a pot of cholent?

There are several factors involved, and a rav should be consulted.

357. What if someone added salt to a pot of food?

- If the pot was not on the fire, the food may be eaten.
- If the pot was on the fire and the salt was the cooked type, the food may be eaten (see Question 74).
- If the pot was on the fire and the salt was the raw type, the status of the food depends on the quantity of salt added. A rav should be consulted.

358. What are the rules for *shehiya*?

There is a penalty in only one situation. If raw food was left on an uncovered fire and by thirteen minutes after sunset was not even edible in an emergency, it may not be eaten by anyone until after Shabbos. In addition, one must wait after Shabbos the length of time that it took to cook the food. There is no difference whether the food was left deliberately or accidentally.

359. What if the mistake was realized after sunset?

The pot of food must be removed from the fire immediately if one estimates that by thirteen minutes after sunset the food will not be edible in an emergency. If the food is *muktzeh* due to it being inedible, one should preferably move it with a *shinuy*. If the food was intended for the day meal, some opinions permit the food to be eaten on Shabbos even if it was not edible by thirteen minutes after sunset.

360. What are the rules for *chazara*?

There is a penalty in the following two cases:
- Hot food was returned to a fire that has no blech.
- Cold food that had not been on a fire on Shabbos was placed on a fire even if there is a blech.

In either case, the food must be removed from the fire as soon as the mistake was realized.

361. What is the penalty in the first case?

- If the taste of the food did not improve by returning it to the fire, there is no penalty.
- If the taste of the food improved by returning it, there is a penalty as follows:
    - If it was done deliberately, no one may eat the food until after Shabbos plus an additional waiting time.
    - If it was done accidentally, the person who did it may not eat the food until after Shabbos plus an additional waiting time. Other people may eat it on Shabbos.

362. What is the penalty in the second case?

If cold food was placed on a fire one must wait until it goes cold, and it may then be eaten by everyone even on Shabbos.

Note: If cold food was placed on a non-adjustable electric hotplate, it may be eaten even hot.

363. What if food was put on a fire and removed immediately?

It may be eaten on Shabbos by everyone since no benefit was gained by the mistake.

364. What are the rules for *hatmana*?

- If the pot was wrapped with *ma'amid hevel* materials, there is no penalty.

- If the pot was wrapped with *mosif hevel* materials, the rules depend on whether it was done before Shabbos or on Shabbos. See the following questions.

365. What if *mosif hevel* materials were used before Shabbos?

- There is a penalty in the following cases:
    - If the food was not edible even in an emergency when it was placed on the fire, it may not be eaten until after Shabbos plus an additional waiting time.
    - If the food was cold and edible when it was placed on the fire, it may be eaten on Shabbos after it has been removed from the fire and left to go cold. It may be reheated on Shabbos in a permitted way.

- There is no penalty in the following cases:
  - The food was hot and edible in an emergency when it was placed on the fire.
  - The food was intended for the day meal.

366. What if *mosif hevel* materials were used on Shabbos?

There is a penalty in the following two cases:

- If the food was hot and its taste was improved by the fire, it may not be eaten until after Shabbos plus an additional waiting time.
- If the food was cold and edible when it was placed on the fire but its taste was not improved by the fire, it may be eaten on Shabbos after it has been removed from the fire and left to go cold. It may be reheated in a permitted way.

367. Is there a difference between deliberate and accidental *hatmana*?

- If the forbidden *hatmana* was deliberate, there is a penalty as explained above.
- If it was accidental, opinions differ whether there is a penalty. One may lenient in times of need.

368. What if opinions differ regarding an act of cooking?

If there is an authoritative opinion that permits a particular act of cooking, there is no penalty. Even if the generally accepted view is to forbid it and therefore one should not do such an act, nevertheless in the event that it was done one may rely on the lenient opinion and not be penalized. This applies to all areas of cooking, i.e. *bishul*, *shehiya*, *chazara*, and *hatmana*.

369. What are examples of dispute in *bishul*?

• Cooking further or hastening the cooking of a food that was edible in an emergency (see Question 15). There is an opinion that this is not a *melacha*, and therefore it may be relied upon if a mistake was made.

• Boiling a food that was already baked or roasted (see Question 30). If one mistakenly put a baked or roasted food into a *kli rishon* off the fire, the food may be eaten on Shabbos since *Sephardic* opinions permit it.

• Reboiling a cold cooked liquid (see Question 25). This is forbidden only by custom, and therefore there is no penalty if it was mistakenly done.

• The laws of a ladle are subject to dispute (see Question 146). One may rely on the lenient opinions if an error occurred; e.g. one poured from a ladle onto rinsed noodles (see Question 152).

• Some opinions do not agree with the concept of a *davar gush* (see Question 159). Therefore, when a mistake happens one may consider a *davar gush* to be a *kli sheini* when transferred once and a *kli shelishi* when transferred twice.

370. What are examples of dispute in *shehiya*?

• Some opinions permit leaving raw food in an oven if the rack beneath it is covered with foil (see Question 204). Although most opinions disagree, the food may be eaten if this was done.

• Opinions differ regarding a cooking appliance that is set with a Shabbos clock to come on during Shabbos (see Question 271).

371. What are examples of dispute in *chazara*?

• Returning food inside an oven if the rack is covered with foil (see Question 258).

• Placing cold cooked food on a hotplate without controls (see Question 268).

• Moving food from an upturned pan to the blech (see Question 287).

• Moving food from area 3 to area 1 or 2 (see Question 289).

372. What is an example of dispute in *hatmana*?

Submerging a wrapped food inside a pot of cholent (see Question 324).

373. May one eat food that was cooked for a dangerously ill person?

When a person's life is in danger, it is permitted to do anything on Shabbos that is necessary including cooking food. Nevertheless, other people may not eat such food until after Shabbos. An additional waiting time is not required.

Glossary

Ashkenaz - German or Polish Jewry.

Blech - Metal sheet used to cover a fire.

Chazal - The Sages.

Chas veshalom - God forbid.

Chazara - Returning food to a fire on Shabbos.

Chutz La'aretz - The Diaspora.

Davar gush - Hot solid food that has been removed from a *kli rishon*.

Ein afiya achar afiya - Baking after baking is not forbidden.

Ein bishul achar bishul - Cooking after cooking is not forbidden.

Eretz Yisroel - The land of Israel.

Erev Shabbos - The day before Shabbos.

Hachana - Preparing for after Shabbos.

Halacha (pl. *Halachos*) - Jewish Law.

Hatmana - Literally, concealing. It refers to the insulation of a pot of hot food by wrapping it with various materials.

Iruy - Literally, pouring. It refers to the pouring of a hot liquid onto a food or another liquid

Kalei habishul - Foods and liquids that cook easily.

Kashei habishul - Foods and liquids that cook with difficulty.

Kli rishon - Literally, a first vessel. It refers to a pot or pan of food or liquid that has been heated by any type of fire.

Kli sheini - Literally, a second vessel. It refers to a hot liquid that was poured directly from a *kli rishon* into a container.

Kli shelishi - Literally, a third vessel. It refers to a hot liquid that was poured directly from a *kli sheini* into a container.

Ma'achal ben drusai - Literally, the food of Ben Drusai. It refers to food that is edible in an emergency.

Ma'amid hevel - A type of material that maintains the food's heat.

Maris ayin - Doing a permitted act that gives the impression to others that a prohibition is being done.

Mav'ir - The *melacha* of making a fire.

Melacha (pl. *melachos*) - Type of constructive act that is forbidden on Shabbos.

Mikveh - Ritual immersion pool.

Mitzvah (pl. *Mitzvos*) - Commandment.

Mishna Brura - The classic and accepted *halachic* work on the daily and holiday laws, written by Rav Yisroel Meir HaCohen Kagan (1839-1933).

Mosif hevel - A type of material that adds heat to the food.

Muktzeh - An item that may not be moved on Shabbos or Yom Tov.

Nireh kimevasheil - An action that resembles cooking.

Sefer (pl. *Sefarim*) - Jewish book.

Sephard - Spanish, Portugese, or North African Jewry.

Shekiya - Sunset.

Shinuy - An unusual action.

Shulchan Aruch - The code of Jewish law.

Talmid Chacham - Torah scholar.

Tzoveya - The *melacha* of dyeing.

Yad soledes bo - Literally, the degree of heat from which the hand withdraws. This refers to the critical temperature at which the *melacha* of bishul can take place.

Yad nichveis bo - A *kli sheini* that is so hot that one's hand would be scalded from it.

Yeish afiya achar bishul - Baking after boiling is forbidden.

Yeish bishul achar afiya - Boiling after baking is forbidden.

Yeish bishul achar bishul - Boiling after boiling is forbidden.

Index

Hebrew Sources
ספרים המובאים במקורות

ארחות שבת - הרב ש.י. גלבר והרב י.מ. רובין.

הלכות שבת במטבח - הרב ש.ב. כהן (ארטסקרול).

הלכות שבת בשבת - הרב מ.מ. קארפ.

זכור ושמור - הרב פ.א. פאלק.

חוט שני - הרב נ. קרליץ.

מאור השבת - הרב מ.מ. יאדלר.

מנחת איש - הרב א.י. שפירא, בני ברק.

מלאכת שבת - הרב י.מ. שטרן.

ספר הלכות שבת - הרב ש. איידר, תשל"ה.

ספר ל"ט מלאכות - הרב ד. ריביאט. הלכות בישול בכרך ג, פרק יא.

שבות יצחק - הרב י. דרזי.

שמירת שבת כהלכתה - הרב י.י. נויוירט, תש"ע.

פרק א - יסודי מלאכת בישול

[1] רמב"ם הלכות שבת פ"ט ה"א, ו, אג"מ או"ח ח"ב סימן פה.
[2] רמב"ם שם, ספר ל"ט מלאכות עמוד 553.   [3] סימן שיח סעיף
יד, רמ"א, שעה"צ ס"ק קיד.   [4] שעה"צ שם.   [5] אג"ט סעיף א,
ב, ועיין אג"מ ח"ג סימן נב שגם ע"י מיקרוגל הוי מלאכה.   [6]
סעיף ג.   [7] סעיף ג, מ"ב ס"ק כא.   [8] שבות יצחק ח"ו עמוד פט
בשם הגרישש"א, מנח"י ח"ד סימן מד אות ג וכ"ד, אז נדברו ח"א
סימן לד, ועיין ששכ"ד פ"א סעיף נא והערה קמה, ועיין ארחות שבת
פ"א הערה רא* שאם המים שבדוד אינם יד סולדת יש מקום
להקל.   [9] סימן שיח סעיף ד, ועיין כה"ח סימן רנג ס"ק כח.   [10]
אג"ט סעיף ד, חזו"א סימן נ סעיף ט ד"ה ויש.   [11] מ"ב סימן רנד
סק"מ.   [12] שו"ע סעיף יד, יז, מ"ב סק"צ.   [13] שם סעיף יד.
[14] מ"ב ס"ק פט, אג"מ ח"ד סימן עד אות ג, שבות יצחק ח"ט
עמוד רח בשם הגרישש"א והגרשז"א.   [15] סעיף ד, מ"ב ס"ק כו,
מסקנת הביה"ל סד"ה אפילו בעודו רותח.   [16] סעיף ד, מ"ב ס"ק
לג, צב.   [17] זכור ושמור עמוד 5.   [18] ששכ"ב פ"א הערה קסט
בשם הגרשז"א שמסתפק, מאור השבת ח"ב סימן ט סעיף יג בשם
כמה פוסקים לכאן ולכאן, הלכות שבת בשבת סעיף עט אוסר.
[21] אג"ט ס"ק יט אות יג, שבה"ש הקדמה לבישול אות יז ד"ה
והנה.   [22] שו"ע סעיף יד, יז, מ"ב סק"צ, סימן שא סעיף מו.   [23]
סימן שא מ"ב ס"ק קסט, ארחות שבת פ"א סעיף י.   [24] אג"ט
השמטה לסעיף ח, מנח"י ח"י סימן כח ד"ה אולם, ששכ"ב פ"א
הערה יז, וע"ע אג"מ ח"ד סימן עד אות א.   [25] רמ"א סעיף טו.
[26] אג"ט סעיף ח, גר"ז סעיף ט, אג"מ ח"ד סימן עד אות ב, וע"ע

[27] חזו"א סימן לז ס"ק יג ד"ה וכתב הרמ"א שמשמע שמקיל טפי וסגי בחמימות ניכרת, ועיין הלכות שבת בשבת פ"ח הערה 163. [29] לענין צנצמים עיין שש"כ פ"א סעיף עא [20] זכור ושמור עמוד 20. בשם הגרשז"א להחמיר, ועיין כה"ח ס"ק עח, וע"ע חוט שני ח"ב עמוד קצא שמתיר. [30] רמ"א סעיף ה, מ"ב ס"ק מז. [31] מ"ב ס"ק מא, קצה"ש סימן קכד ס"ק נד מ"ב ס"ק מא, קצה"ש סימן קכד ס"ק נד. [32] מנח"ש ח"א סימן י אות ג, ארחות שבת סעיף לד. [33] זכור ושמור עמוד 22-21. [34] שם, ספר ל"ט מלאכות הערה 161a, מנחת איש פ"ה הערה 206, ועיין שבה"ל ח"ז סימן יב אות ד. [35] ערוה"ש סעיף נז, זכור ושמור שם, ספר ל"ט מלאכות שם, וכ"כ במ"ב מהדורת דרשו אות 54 לפי החזו"א וכף החיים ס"ק עח. [36] זכור ושמור שם. [37] תהל"ד ס"ק כד, חזו"א סימן לז סוף סעיף יד, ארחות שבת סעיף יט. [38] אג"ט סוף סעיף ט, מאור השבת ח"ב עמוד צא בשם הגריש"א. [40] ביה"ל סעיף ה ד"ה יש, מאור השבת ח"ב עמוד קץ בשם הגרשז"א ושם עמוד קנו הערה צז. [41] שם הערה קא בשם הרבה פוסקים, שזה נחשב להמשך הבישול. [42] ביה"ל שם.

פרק ב - ממהר הבישול

[43] מאירי שבת עג/א במנין המלאכות אות יא, רעק"א ריש סימן שיח, מ"ב ס"ק קיד, שעה"צ ס"ק קלז. [44] זכור ושמור עמוד 7, דינים והנהגות חזו"א פי"ג סעיף יג, ועיין שבות יצחק דיני בישול פמ"ב אות ב שיש ספק אם זה מעשה בישול גמור או גרמא, וע"ע שש"כ פ"א הערה קי שהגרשז"א הסתפק אם יש לחשוש כשהמים כבר יד סולדת. [45] סימן רנד סעיף ד, ועיין ערוה"ש סימן רנד סעיף י שיש ליזהר מאד לא להחזיר המכסה. [46] פשוט. [47] ערוה"ש שם. [48] מאור השבת ח"א סימן ב סעיף כח, מלאכת שבת עמוד קיג. [49] רמ"א סו"ס רנט. [50] מ"ב ס"ק כד. [51] סימן שיח סעיף יח, מ"ב ס"ק קיד, סימן רנז סעיף ד, ביה"ל ד"ה גורם. [52] מ"ב סימן שיח ס"ק קיז. [53] סעיף יח, מ"ב ס"ק קטו, אג"מ ח"ד סימן עד אות יא, שבות יצחק ח"ט עמוד תל בשם הגריש"א, וע"ע הלכות שבת בשבת פד שמקיל להוציא מאכל מקדירה שעומד על בלער. [54] לענין הזזה, פשוט. לענין כיסוי עיין מאור השבת ח"ב סימן י ס"ק מח בשם הרבה פוסקים, וע"ע אג"מ ח"ד סימן עד אות י (ולכ' מפורש להתיר במ"ב סימן רנד ס"ק כג). לענין הגסה עיין מ"ב ס"ק קיג, וע"ע חזו"א סימן לז סעיף טו. לענין הוצאה בכף עיין מ"ב ס"ק קיג ועי"ע חזו"א סימן לז סעיף טו. [55] מאור השבת ח"ב עמוד שלט בשם הגריש"א והגרשז"א שמתירים לחתוך ולהוציא קוגל שעומד ע"ג האש, אג"מ ח"ד סימן עד אות יד. ולגבי הוצאת מאכל מחלק העליון עיין חוט שני ח"ב עמוד קצה שמתיר להוציא גוש שיושב למעלה מן הרוטב ואוסר מתוך הרוטב,

ועיין שבות יצחק ח"ט עמוד תכח בשם הגריש"א שמותר להוציא אם יזהר שלא לעשות מעט עירוב, ועיין הלכות שבת בשבת עמוד תקכב ומנחת איש סעיף סח. [56] שו"ת אבני נזר או"ח סימן נט אות ה שדוקא מים, וכ"כ במאור השבת ח"ב עמוד תרטו הערה קפ בשם הגרשז"א ובזכור ושמור עמוד 9. אבל בחוט שני ח"ב עמוד קצו כ' להתיר, וכ"כ בהלכות שבת במטבח עמוד 48, וכ"כ בספר ל"ט מלאכות עמוד 560. [57] אג"מ ח"ד סימן עד אות ט, וע"ע אז נדברו ח"ה סימן יג. [58] אג"מ ח"ד סימן עד אות יא. [59] שבות יצחק ח"ט עמוד תלא ותלב בשם הגריש"א, ארחות שבת פ"א סעיף צה. [60] מנח"י ח"ח סימן כה, מבית לוי ח"ו עמוד לה, חוט שני ח"ב עמוד קנב, וע"ע מאור השבת ח"ב סימן ט סעיף י שיש אוסרים לגמרי ויש מתירים לגמרי. אז נדברו ח"ט סימן יג, הלכות שבת בשבת פ"ח הערה 141 בשם הגריש"א.

פרק ג - כלי ראשון

[61] סעיף ט. [62] אג"ט סעיף יב, חוט שני ח"ב עמוד קצו אות ח. [63] חיי"א כלל כ סימן ג, סימן שיח סעיף ט, יא. [64] שש"כ סעיף מה, ארחות שבת סעיף צט. [65] שם בהערה*. [66] שם סעיף ק. ארחות שבת הערה קצט, ספר ל"ט מלאכות עמוד 641, מבית לוי ח"ו עמוד מ. [67] ארחות שבת עמודים נו-נח, ספר ל"ט מלאכות עמוד 666, שש"כ פל"ז סעיף טו. [68] שם. [69] מ"ב ס"ק לג ויל"ע במש"כ השעה"צ שעיקר סיבת האיסור משום שיש בישול אחר בישול על האש, בשם האי"ר, הלא חומרת האי"ר משום הגסה, וכן הקשה בספר הלכות שבת עמוד 313. [70] רמ"א סעיף ה, מ"ב שם. [71] מ"ב ס"ק סט, לב, מאור השבת ח"ב עמוד נב בשם הרבה פוסקים, ועיין הלכות שבת בשבת פ"ח הערה 176. [72] עיין מ"ב ס"ק ק, קג וה"ה בנד"ד. [73] מ"ב ס"ק עא ושעה"צ ס"ק צו, ועיין רעק"א על המג"א ס"ק לא. והחילוק בין שומן לסוכר עיין חוט שני ח"ב עמוד קפז ד"ה איברא. [74] סעיף ט, מ"ב שם. ועיין במדריך הבד"ץ שנת תשע"ה עמוד 58 שכ' שהיום כל סוגי המלח אינם מבושלים בא"י. [75] הלכות שבת במטבח עמוד 34, זכור ושמור עמוד 20, שש"כ הערה קצט. [76] סעיף יא, רמ"א סעיף טו. [77] אג"מ ח"א סימן צג ד"ה והנה עירוי, וח"ד סימן עד אות יט, מנח"י ח"ט סימן לא, שבה"ש הקדמה לבישול אות יט, שבות יצחק ח"ט עמוד שצח בשם הגריש"א. [78] מנחת איש פ"ה סעיף ק. [79] שש"כ סעיף סו, מאור השבת ח"א סימן ג סעיף יט. [80] מבית לוי ח"ו עמוד כו אות ז, מאור השבת שם הערה לה, ועיין שו"ע סימן שא סעיף מו ומ"ב שם. [81] רמ"א סעיף יד, מ"ב ס"ק צא. [82] סעיף יד, מ"ב סק"צ וס"ק קח, ועיין הלכות שבת בשבת הערה 111 שהחיי"א התיר להפשיר דבר לח שכבר נתבשל שלא מחמירינן שמא ישכח מליטלו משם מחלוקת אם יבא"ב, והגריש"א אמר

שיש לסמוך ע"ז בשעת הדחק.   [83] מנח"י ח"ט סימן לא, מאור
השבת ח"ב עמוד תרי"ב בשם הגרשז"א, ועיין ארחות שבת פ"ג
סעיף קיז שיתכן שיש בזה איסור בורר, וכן עורר בשבות יצחק ח"ט
עמוד תא, וע"ע במנחת איש סעיף קג אוסר להוריד הקרח, וצ"ע.
[84] מ"ב ס"ק סט, לב, מאור השבת ח"ב עמוד נב בשם הרבה
פוסקים, ועיין הלכות שבת בשבת פ"ח הערה 176.   [85] סעיף טז,
מ"ב ס"ק קה.   [86] מאור השבת ח"ב עמוד קסח בשם פוסקים.
[87] מאור השבת ח"א סימן ג סעיף כ והערה לו, זכור ושמור עמוד
10.   [88] לענין בישול עיין סימן שיח סעיף יב ומ"ב סק"פ. לענין
הכנה עיין שש"כ פי"ב סעיף ג שמתיר, ועיין מאור השבת ח"א סימן
ג' הערה כט בשם הגרי"י פישר לאסור, ועיין ספר ל"ט מלאכות
עמוד 120.   [89] מ"ב ס"ק סד.

פרק ד - כלי שני

[90] מ"ב ס"ק פז.   [91] שבת מ/ב תוס' ד"ה וש"מ, מ"ב ס"ק מב.
[92] אג"ט סעיף טז, גר"ז סעיף יב.   [93] שבה"ש סק"ע, שש"כ פ"א
ס"ק קעד, מ"ב ס"ק מב, ט"ז סק"ח, אג"מ ח"ד סימן עד אות יח.
[94] סעיף ט, רמ"א, מ"ב ס"ק עא.   [95] שעה"צ ס"ק סח, סעיף יג,
שש"כ הערה קעג.   [96] מ"ב סוף ס"ק לט, שש"כ סעיף סא, מנח"י
ח"ה סימן קכז אות ה.   [97] רמ"א סעיף ה, הלכות שבת בשבת
פ"ח סעיף פ, שש"כ סעיף סח.   [98] מ"ב ס"ק עא, אג"מ ח"ד סעיף
עד אות טז.   [99] מאור השבת ח"ב סימן יא סעיף כד וח"ג סימן יג
הערה מד, שש"כ פ"א הערה קפב, קפו*, קפה*, מדריך כשרות
לבד"ץ עדה החרדית תשע"ה עמוד 58.   [100] אג"מ שם, ספר
הלכות שבת עמוד 298 הערה תמב, מדריך כשרות לבד"ץ עדה
החרדית תשע"ה עמוד 58, ארחות שבת הערה קעח בשם
הגריש"א, שבות יצחק ח"ח עמוד רצה בשם הגרי"ש. ושמענו
מאת הגר"י מורגנשטרן שהגריש"א אמר כמה פעמים שאין לחשוש
שהקליה הקלה שעושים לקפה נגמר בסוף הייצור עושה בעיה של
בישול אחר אפייה אחר בישול.   [101] מאור השבת ח"ב סימן יא
סק"א, שש"כ הערה קפד, קפה*.   [102] מדריך כשרות לבד"ץ עדה
החרדית תשע"ה עמוד 58, ארחות שבת סעיף מח.   [103] בצל
החכמה ח"ב סימן עד אות ב, ארחות שבת פ"א סעיף פד, הלכות
שבת בשבת פ"ח סעיף לז, ועיין שבות יצחק ח"ט עמוד עה
שהגריש"א חשש שדינו ככלי ראשון שניתן לבשל בתוכו, אבל
עירוי ממנו אינו נחשב כעירוי מכלי ראשון.   [104] זכור ושמור
עמוד 11.   [105] פרמ"ג א"א סימן רנג ס"ק לב.   [106] מאור השבת
ח"א סימן ג סעיף יד ע"פ מג"א סימן רנז ס"ק יד.   [107] חיי"א כלל
כ סימן ד, מ"ב סק מח, ביה"ל סימן שיט סעיף ד ד"ה חייב, חזו"א
סימן נב ס"ק יט ד"ה וכל.   [108] חזו"א שם, זכור ושמור עמוד 27.
[109] שבה"ל ח"ז סימן מב סוף אות א.   [110] ארחות שבת סעיף נז

והערה קמ, מאור השבת ח"א עמוד קצח בשם הגרח"ק, זכור ושמור עמוד 27. [111] סעיף יג, שעה"צ ס"ק סח. [112] שבות יצחק עמוד צד בשם הגריש"א. [113] עיין מקורות 12, 22. [114] מ"ב ס"ק סד.

פרק ה - כלי שלישי

[115] פשוט. [116] סעיף ד, מ"ב ס"ק לו, ביה"ל ד"ה חרץ וד"ה וקולייס, שש"כ סעיף סג, הלכות שבת בשבת סעיף מ, זכור ושמור עמוד 12, וע"ע אג"מ ח"ד סימן עד אות טו שמתיר בתה. [117] חזו"א סימן נב ס"ק יט, שבה"ל ח"ז סימן מב סוף אות א, וע"ע שבות יצחק עמוד צט בשם הגריש"א. [118] מ"ב ס"ק סד, וע"ע שבות יצחק עמוד שו בשם הגריש"א. [119] פשוט, ועיין חזו"א סימן נט סעיף יט בסוף שכ' שאין מקור לחלק בין שני לשלישי, וא"כ לדידן שנוהגין לחלק מ"מ אין מקור לחלק בין שלישי לרביעי, וע"ע שבות יצחק עמוד שו בשם הגריש"א. [120] מלאכת שבת עמוד קו ד"ה ואם. [121] שש"כ סעיף נה, נב. [122] שם סעיף נג, ועיין ארחות שבת הערה קסא שחושש שההתמצית אינו מבושל כ"צ ע"י עירוי מקומקום בער"ש, וכ"כ בזכור ושמור עמוד 33 שלכן בשבת מותר להכניס התמצית רק בכלי שני או שלישי. [123] זכור ושמור דש עמוד 9, ארחות שבת סעיף עח. [124] ארחות שבת פ"ג סעיף עט. [125] שבות יצחק עמוד שיד בשם הגריש"א, ספר הלכות שבת עמוד 294. לכאורה זה אינו מובן, כי טעם התמצית שיצא במים הקרים אינו מבושל והוי לן לאסרו בכלי שני. [126] לגבי קפה שחור שאינו עובר תהליך בישול, אם מותר להכניסו בכלי שלישי עיין אג"מ ח"ד סימן עד אות יח שמתיר, וכן משמע בשש"כ סעיף סח, אבל עיין אז נדברו ח"ט סימן יב, וארחות שבת סעיף פה שאוסרים, ועיין הלכות שבת בשבת הערה 195 ושבות יצחק עמוד רצד.

פרק ו - עירוי

[128] סעיף י, מ"ב ס"ק עד, פב, לט. [129] שש"כ סעיף נב, נה. [130] אג"מ ח"ד סימן עד אות יט, שבה"ש הקדמה לביטול אות יט. [131] שש"כ סעיף פג והערה רמו, זכור ושמור עמוד 29. [132] סעיף יב. [133] שש"כ סעיף נו. [134] סעיף יד, שעה"צ ס"ק סח. [135] שש"כ סעיף סב. [136] פרמ"ג א"א ס"ק לה, מ"ב ס"ק לה, לו. [137] שש"כ סעיף סג. [138] שבות יצחק עמוד ק בשם הגריש"א. [139] ספר ל"ט מלאכות עמוד 654, ועיי"ש שיש בזה גם איסור מוליד. [140] מ"ב סימן שכ ס"ק נו, שעה"צ סימן שיח ס"ק סה. [141] מ"ב שם, הליכות שלמה מועדים (פסח) פ"ט סעיף ה. [142] שו"ת רב פעלים ח"ג סימן יא, וע"ע קצות השלחן סימן קמו ס"ק יד שכ' טעם ההיתר משום שינוי. [143] שש"כ פי"א סעיף לט. [144] ספר ל"ט מלאכות עמוד 662, הלכות שבת לבית לרב שמחה בונים

כהן עמוד 337, זכור ושמור צובע עמוד 7. [145] שעה"צ סימן שיח ס"ק סה.

פרק ז - המצקת

[146] ט"ז יו"ד סימן צב סק"ל ואו"ח סימן שיח ס"ק יט, מג"א סימן תנב סק"ט, מ"ב סימן שיח ס"ק פז. [147] ארחות שבת סעיף עג, זכור ושמור עמוד 14, ספר ל"ט מלאכות עמוד 581, ספר הלכות שבת עמוד 290. [148] הלכות שבת במטבח עמוד 36. [149] פשוט, ולא מצאנו מפורש. [150] מ"ב ס"ק מה, ארחות שבת הערה קסג. [151] ספר ל"ט מלאכות עמוד 582, שש"כ הערה רי. [152] פשוט. [153] מ"ב סימן רנג ס"ק פד, ארחות שבת הערה קסב. [154] עיין מ"ב ס"ק פז שדינו ודאי ככלי ראשון אם מעלה רתיחה, וברור דמיירי בכ"ר שעל האש ולא על השלחן שא"א להעלות רתיחה שם, וכ"כ בארחות שבת הערה קסא ומאור השבת ח"א עמוד רמ"ד ד"ה ומה, ומנחת איש פ"ה סעיף ס, וכמה מחברים טעו בדיוק זה והחמירו שלא לצורך. [155] שמענו מאת הגרי"י נויברט. [156] מאור השבת שם, חזו"א סימן קכב סק"ג ד"ה סדר, ארחות שבת הערה קסב. [157] שבה"ש סעיף כא, וע"ע חזו"א סימן קכב סק"ג ד"ה סדר שכ' שהמצקת עצמה היא כלי שלישי.

פרק ח - דבר גוש

[158] יש"ש חולין פ"ח סוף סימן עא. [159] שם, ש"ך יו"ד סימן קה סק"ח, מג"א סימן שיח ס"ק מה, מ"ב ס"ק מה. [160] מ"ב שם, זכור ושמור עמוד 15, אג"מ ח"ד סימן עד אות ה. [161] מ"ב ס"ק סה, ועיין יד יהודה יו"ד סימן קה בפירוש הארוך ס"ק יד. [162] שבות יצחק עמוד קמט, וע"ע חוט שני ח"ב עמוד קפג. [163] ש"ך יו"ד סימן קה סוף סק"ח, פ"ת סימן צד סק"ז, הלכות שבת בשבת סעיף נא. [164] פשוט. [165] פשוט, ויש לעיין אם דינו עכשיו ככלי שלישי. [166] עיין מאור השבת ח"א עמוד ערב בשם הגרשי"א, ונראה שזו כוונתו, וע"ע תורת המלאכות (לייטנר) ח"ב עמוד קמא בשם הגרנ"ק שאפילו אם אין כולו בתוך הרוטב לא מקרי דבר גוש [אבל אין להקל בזה למעשה], וכ"כ בספר ל"ט מלאכות עמוד 584, וצ"ע. [167] מ"ב ס"ק סה. [168] מאור השבת ח"א סימן ו ס"ק יג וח"ג סימן יג הערה לו, ועיי"ש שתמה על מ"ש באג"מ ח"ד סימן עד אות ה. [169] מאור השבת ח"א סימן ו סעיף יג. [170] פשוט, וידוע שפיסטור של ביצים נעשה בלי בישול. [171] שש"כ הערה קצח בשם הגרשז"א אוסר, ואג"מ ח"ד סימן עד אות ו מתיר. [172] אג"מ ח"ד סימן עד אות ה, שש"כ סעיף סד, הלכות שבת בשבת הערה 100 בשם הגרשי"א. [173] הלכות שבת בשבת הערה 105, זכור ושמור עמוד 30, חוט שני ח"ב עמוד קסג, ויש אוסרים בזה דהוי כעירוי כלי ראשון וגרע מהנחת רוטב על דבר גוש שכבר נמצא בכלי שני, וכן משמע במ"ב ס"ק עח, וכן

פסקו בשש"כ הערה קצו וארחות שבת סעיף סב, ועיין שעה"צ ס"ק קח שהעיר בעצמו שיש מפקפקין ע"ז, ושמעענו מהגר"צ ובר שיש להקל.   [174] עיין חת"ס סו"ס שיח שדבר גוש מבשל כצלי, מאור השבת ח"א סימן ו ס"ק כד, שש"כ סוף הערה רא.   [175] עיין מאור השבת ח"א סימן ו והערה טו ובם כמה פוסקים להחמיר ודעת הגרשז"א להקל, ודבריהם הובאו ג"כ בארחות שבת הערה קמז, ועיין שש"כ סעיף סה.   [176] מאור השבת סימן ו סעיף יג.   [177] כן נראה.   [178] מאור השבת ח"ג סימן יג סעיף כא.   [179] מאור השבת סימן ו סעיף ה בשם כמה פוסקים.   [180] פשוט.

פרק ט - שהייה (סימן רנג)

[181] סימן רנג סעיף א.   [182] שם.   [183] שם, אג"מ ח"א סימן צג וכן המנהג, וע"ע חזו"א סימן לז סעיף יא.   [184] רמב"ם פרק ג הלכה ד, כסף משנה שם בשם הרמ"ך, לבוש סעיף א.   [185] שש"כ הערה ריז בשם הגרשז"א, שבות יצחק ח"ב עמוד לו בשם הגריש"א.   [186] מאור השבת ח"ב עמוד תרכח בשם הגרשז"א, אג"מ שם ד"ה ולפי"ז, שבה"ל ח"א סימן צא.   [187] זכור ושמור עמוד 40.   [188] שם עמוד 38, שש"כ הערה סג*.   [189] מ"ב ס"ק יד, שבות יצחק ח"ב עמוד לה.   [190] זכור ושמור עמוד 39, שבות יצחק שם, וכן משמע במ"ב הנ"ל.   [191] אג"מ שם.   [192] אג"מ ח"ד סימן עד אות כה.   [193] סימן רנד סעיף ט, מ"ב ס"ק מט. [194] חזו"א סימן לז ס"ק כז ד"ה רנ"ז, חוט שני ח"ב עמוד קו, ארחות שבת פ"ב הערה יא, וע"ע הלכות שבת בשבת פ"ה הערה 14.   [195] רמ"א סימן רנג סעיף א, חזו"א סימן לז סק"ג ד"ה במ"ב, כה"ח ס"ק כח, ביה"ל ד"ה ונהגו.   [196] מ"ב סק"ו.   [197] מנחת שלמה ח"ג סימן יב אות ד.   [198] אג"מ ח"ד סימן עד אות כד, ארחות שבת פ"ב הערה ח, הלכות שבת במטבח עמוד 55.   [199] ספר הלכות שבת עמוד 334, ספר ל"ט מלאכות עמוד 609, שש"כ סעיף עב.   [200] שם.   [201] ספר הלכות שבת עמוד 380.   [202] ספר הלכות שבת עמוד 380, שבות יצחק ח"ב עמוד לו אות ה. [203] חוט שני ח"ב עמוד קיג.   [204] שבות יצחק ח"ב עמוד לו בשם הגריש"א, חוט שני עמוד קיב.   [205] מנחת איש פ"ו סעיף ט, פסק"ת סימן רנג הערה 74, ועיין ארחות שבת פכ"ו הערה כה. [206] עיין ארחות שבת פכ"ו סעיף טו והערה ז, מבית לוי ח"ו עמוד לג סעיף ח, זכור ושמור עמוד 51, שבות יצחק חי"ב עמוד קיז בשם הגריש"א, שש"כ סעיף לה, וע"ע אג"מ ח"ד סימן עד אות כח שמתיר בשעה שהאש נסגר.   [207] פשוט, וכ"כ זכור ושמור שם. [208] ארחות שבת פכ"ו סעיף ד לענין מקרר, וה"ה תנור מאותו טעם, עיי"ש בהערה ח.   [209] עיין זכור ושמור עמוד 49.   [210] שש"כ סעיף כט-ל, ספר ל"ט מלאכות עמוד 613, זכור ושמור עמוד 40, ארחות שבת פ"ב סעיף יג, ועיי"ש שלדעת הגריש"א ח' כיסוי

משום לא פלוג. [211] ספר ל"ט מלאכות עמוד 614, זכור ושמור
עמוד 55, הלכות שבת במטבח עמוד 53, וע"ע שם עמוד 56 בשם
הגר"י הענקין שמתיר להשהות בשר חי בלי בלער אם לא יתבשל
בזמן סעודת ערב. [212] שם. [213] עיין מאור השבת ח"ב עמוד
תרט"ז בשם הגרשי"א ושבות יצחק ח"ב עמוד צו בשם הגריש"א
שצריך נייר עבה, ועיין זכור ושמור עמוד 39 שא"צ עבה, ועיין ספר
ל"ט מלאכות עמוד 613 והלכות שבת במטבח עמוד 53, ומבית לוי
ח"ו עמוד לג שכולם הזכירו נייר כסף סתם בלי להדגיש שצריך
עבה. [214] זכור ושמור עמוד 56, ארחות שבת פ"ב סעיף כח.
[215] שם, שם סעיף כט. [216] שם ושם. [217] מאור השבת ח"ד
סימן יד סק"ל, מטבח כהלכה (מורגנשטרן) עמוד 177 הערה 11.
[218] שש"כ סעיף מו, ארחות שבת פ"ב סעיף לא. [219] ארחות
שבת שם. [220] שבות יצחק ח"ב עמוד קמח בשם הגריש"א
והגרשז"א, הובא ג"כ בארחות שבת פ"ב סעיף לד. [221] זכור
ושמור עמוד 58. [222] שם עמוד 59.

פרק י - חזרה (סימן רנג)

[223] סעיף ב. [224] מ"ב ס"ק נה, פז. [225] מ"ב ס"ק לז. [226]
סעיף ב, רמ"א. [227] מ"ב ס"ק לז, נו, ועיין ספר הלכות שבת עמוד
352 הערה תתקמז. [228] שבות יצחק עמוד רל ע"פ אור שמח
רפ"ג דהלכות שבת. [229] גר"ז סעיף יד. [230] רמ"א סעיף ב,
מ"ב ס"ק סב. [231] אג"מ ח"ד סימן עד אות כט, ספר הלכות שבת
עמוד 340, שש"כ סעיף כ בהגה"ה והערה סו. [232] שם, ועיין
סעיף ג. [233] עיין מקורות לשאלה הבאה. [234] ספר הלכות
שבת עמוד 353 הערה תתקמח, הלכות שבת במטבח עמוד 62,
זכור ושמור עמוד 42, וע"ע אבי עזרי הלכות שבת פרק ג הלכה י,
ארחות שבת פ"ב הערה עח באריכות ומסיק שנחלקו בזה הגריש"א
והגריש"א. [235] פשוט. [236] עיין שש"כ סעיף כ אות ד, הלכות
שבת במטבח עמוד 61, ספר ל"ט מלאכות עמוד 619, זכור ושמור
עמוד 43 שהקילו, ועיין שבות יצחק עמוד קסא בשם הגריש"א
שהחמיר. [237] חוט שני ח"ב עמוד קכג אות ב, מנחת איש פ"ו
סעיף כט, וע"ע הלכות שבת בשבת פ"ה סעיף ח. [238] משמעות
לשונו של מנחת איש שכ' "ואמר לו לאוחזו בידיו עד שיחזירנה",
וכן נראה כי לאדם השני נראה כנתינה חדשה כי לא היתה לו
כוונה מתחילה. [239] פשוט, וכתבנו מפני הטועים. [240] מ"ב
ס"ק נד. [241] ביה"ל סעיף ה ד"ה ובלבד, חזו"א סימן לז סק"י ד"ה
ואם, אג"ט סק"נ אות ג, וע"ע אג"מ ח"ד סימן עד אות לא. [242]
עיין גר"ז סעיף יד, מנח"י ח"ו סימן כ, שבה"ל ח"ג סימן צג אות ב,
אג"מ ח"ד סימן סט, זכור ושמור עמוד 46 שאוסרים. ועיין שעה"צ
ס"ק מז, שש"כ הערה מט ומאור השבת ח"א עמוד תקב בשם
הגרשז"א, ארחות שבת פ"ב סעיף נט, חוט שני עמוד קכה שמתירין.

[243] כן נראה, וכ"כ בשבות יצחק עמוד רד בשם הגריש"א. [244]
שש"כ סעיף יז, זכור ושמור עמוד 46, שבות יצחק שם, ארחות שבת
פ"א הערה קצו. [245] הלכות שבת במטבח עמוד 68. [246] ספר
ל"ט מלאכות עמוד 617. [247] לענין הבלוע עיין מ"ב ס"ק נב,
לענין הצטנן עיין ביה"ל סעיף ה ד"ה ובלבד, לענין כלי שני סומכים
על שעה"צ ס"ק מז. [248] מ"ב ס"ק נו. [249] שם, ביה"ל ד"ה ולא
הניחם, חוט שני ח"ב עמוד קכג אות ד, ולענין הנחה ע"ג השיש
עיין ארחות שבת הערה או שהרבה פוסקים מדמים לכסא ולא
לקרקע ודלא כשבה"ל. [250] מ"ב ס"ק סה, סז, שש"כ הערה עד.
[251] עיין שבה"ש ס"ק מז, שש"כ הערה עה בשם הגרשז"א,
הלכות שבת במטבח עמוד 66 הערה 17 בשם הגרחפ"ש שמקילין,
ועיין שבות יצחק עמוד קעד בשם הגריש"א, מנחת איש הערה 70
בשם הגרנ"ק שמחמירין, ועיין מבית לוי ח"ח עמוד כא סעיף כ
שחילק כמו שכתבנו. [252] שש"כ הערה עט בשם הגרשז"א,
אג"מ ח"ד סימן עד אות לח, ארחות שבת פ"ב הערה פא, ועיי"ש
הערה פב שדעת הגריש"א והגרנ"ק להתיר רק אם הבלוע לא
הצטנן. [253] ספר ל"ט מלאכות עמוד 1280, הלכות שבת לבית
עמוד 471. [254] מבית לוי ח"ו עמוד לב סעיף ז. [255] שש"כ
פל"ב הערה קפב בשם הגרשז"א, ארחות שבת פ"ב הערה פג, וע"ע
מנחת איש פ"ו סעיף מג. [256] מאור השבת ח"א עמוד תצה בשם
הגרשז"א, שש"כ סעיף כח. [257] מ"ב ס"ק צ ושעה"צ ס"ק פח.
[258] שש"כ סעיף יט, מנח"י ח"ג סימן כח, שבות יצחק עמוד פט
בשם הגריש"א, אג"מ ח"ד סימן עד אות כז, זכור ושמור עמוד 45,
וע"ע שבה"ל ח"ג סימן מח ובספר הלכות שבת עמוד 354 הערה
תתקסג בשם הגר"א קוטלר שהתירו. [259] פשוט. [260] פשוט.
[261] אג"מ ח"ד סימן עד אות לח, וכן שמענו מאת הגר"ח ובר.
[262] פשוט. [263] פשוט. [264] עיין מקורות 252. [265] חזו"א
סימן לז ס"ק טו סד"ה סימן, ואע"פ שהתיר אפילו לכתחילה, עיין
מ"ב סימן שיח שיח ס"ק קיג שאסר לכתחילה, וכ"כ בשבות יצחק ח"ט
עמוד תלג בשם הגריש"א שלכתחילה יש לסדר תבשילו באופן
אחר. [266] כן נראה פשוט דלא מקרי חזרה אם מקצתו עדיין על
האש, ועיין זכור ושמור עמוד 46, ועיין הלכות שבת בשבת פ"ה
סעיף ה. [267] הלכות שבת במטבח עמוד 60, מנחת איש פ"ו
סעיף ח, ספר ל"ט מלאכות עמוד 626. [268] עיין יבי"א ח"ו סימן
לב ומאור השבת ח"א עמוד תצו שהספרדים מתירים, וע"ע אג"מ
ח"ד סימן עד אות לה שמתיר אם א"א להתבשל שם; ועיין שש"כ
סעיף ל, הר צבי או"ח סימן קלו, זכור ושמור עמוד 54, הלכות שבת
במטבח עמוד 60 שדינו כאש מכוסה; ועיין שבות יצחק ח"ב עמוד
צו בשם הגריש"א וחוט שני עמוד קיד שצריך כיסוי משום לא פלוג.
[269] זכור ושמור עמוד 55, הלכות שבת במטבח עמוד 60, ספר

ל"ט מלאכות עמוד 614, וע"ע ארחות שבת הערה קמט שמסתפק
אם מותר להחזיר בו. [270] זכור ושמור עמוד 57. [271] עיין ספר
הלכות שבת עמוד 322, 323 באריכות, ומאור השבת ח"ד סימן יד
סעיף לו, לז, שבות יצחק ח"ב פ"ט. [272] מאור השבת שם סעיף
לח בשם הגרשי"א. [273] זכור ושמור עמוד 53, הלכות שבת
במטבח עמוד 221, וע"מ אג"מ ח"ד סימן ס שמתנגד לכל שימוש
בשעון שבת. [274] מ"ב סימן רנג ס"ק נה, פז. [275] סעיף ה, מ"ב
סק"צ, ספר הלכות שבת עמוד 313, סימן שיח סעיף טו. [276] מ"ב
סימן רנג ס"ק פה. [277] ספר הלכות שבת עמוד 313. [278] חוט
שני ח"ב עמוד קל אות ב (השני). [279] אג"מ ח"א סימן צג ד"ה
ובדבר תנור. [280] עיין שש"כ פ"א הערה קכו, שבה"ל ח"א סימן
צא, ספר ל"ט מלאכות עמוד 621 שמתירין, ועיין שבות יצחק עמוד
נט בשם הגרשי"א, אז נדברו ח"ג סימן יד, חוט שני ח"ב עמוד קכט
ד"ה ונראה שאוסרין. [281] עיין שש"כ שם שכ' צלחת, וכ"כ
בספר ל"ט מלאכות עמוד 621. [282] שש"כ שם, סימן שח סעיף ג
ומ"ב ס"ק יב. [283] פשוט. [284] עיין חזו"א סימן לז סק"ח ד"ה
הא. [285] אג"מ ח"ד סימן סא וח"א סימן צד, שש"כ סעיף כה,
ארחות שבת פ"ב סעיף סב אות א, וע"ע שם סעיף סט אות ב.
[286] חזו"א סימן לז ס"ק יא, שש"כ סעיף מד, שבה"ל ח"א סימן
צא. [287] פשוט. [288] כן נראה. [289] אג"מ ח"א סימן צד, חוט
שני ח"ב עמוד קלב ד"ה ואמנם, זכור ושמור עמוד 47, מנחת איש
פ"ו סעיף מו, וע"ע שבות יצחק עמוד עד בשם הגרשי"א. [290]
פשוט. [291] פשוט. [292] אג"מ ח"ד סימן סא וסימן עד אות יב
לפי הבנת ר' ספר הלכות שבת בספר הלכות שבת עמוד 365, וכ"כ
בשבות יצחק עמוד עז והלכות שבת במטבח עמוד 45. [293]
פשוט.

פרק יא - הטמנה (סימן רנז)

[294] מ"ב סק"א. [295] סעיף ג. [296] סעיף ח, ביה"ל סימן רנח
ד"ה מותר. [297] סעיף א, מ"ב סק"ו, סעיף ה, מ"ב סק"ל, סעיף ו.
[298] סעיף א, ה. [299] מ"ב סימן רסא ס"ק כח, הלכות שבת
בשבת פ"ה סעיף כד. [300] פשוט, עיין סימן רסא סעיף ד ומ"ב
ס"ק כח. [301] סימן רנז סעיף ד, מ"ב ס"ק כה. [302] שם, מ"ב
ס"ק כו. [303] ערוה"ש סעיף כ, גר"ז סעיף ח. [304] מ"ב ס"ק כה.
[305] רמ"א סימן רנג סוף סעיף א, סימן רנז סעיף ח, וע"ע חזו"א
סימן לז ס"ק יט ד"ה כתב במ"ב סי' רנ"ג. [306] מ"ב סימן רנג ס"ק
מח, סט, שבות יצחק עמוד רמז בשם הגרשז"א, וע"ע שם בשם
הגרשי"א שצריך כשליש מגולה, וע"ע אג"מ ח"ד סימן עד אות ד
שצריך לגלות מקום המאכל דוקא ולא די בגילוי המכסה. [307]
פשוט. [308] פשוט. [309] ארחות שבת פ"ב סעיף פה. [310]
שעה"צ סימן רנז ס"ק מג, ארחות שבת פ"ב סעיף פד. [311]

פסק"ת סימן רנז הערה 14, וכן מוכח מדין 313. [312] הלכות שבת
במטבח עמוד 79, זכור ושמור עמוד 67. [313] סעיף ח, מ"ב ס"ק
מב, שעה"צ ס"ק מג. [314] מ"ב ס"ק מד. [315] עיין ביה"ל סימן
רנז סעיף ו ד"ה אפילו, שדבר חם שהולך ומתקרר נידון כמעמיד
הבל בע"ש וכמוסיף הבל בשבת. [316] חזו"א סימן לז ס"ק לב ד"ה
והר"ן, אג"מ ח"א סימן צה, קצה"ש סימן עא ס"ק לו, וע"ע שבה"ל
ח"א סימן צג. [317] זכור ושמור עמוד 66. [318] ארחות שבת
סעיף עה, הלכות שבת במטבח עמוד 76 ועיי"ש בהערה 13 מ"ש
בשם שבה"ל ח"ה סימן ל. [319] מ"ב סימן רנח סק"ב. [320]
הלכות שבת במטבח עמוד 81. [321] שבות יצחק עמוד רנז בשם
הגריש"א, מבית לוי ח"ו עמוד לו אות ב, שו"ת מחזה אליהו סימן
לב, וע"ע אג"מ ח"ד סימן עד אות ג שאוסר, ועיין מאור השבת ח"א
עמוד תצד בשם הגרשז"א שאם הכוונה לשמור החום אסור ואם
כדי למנוע התפוררות מותר. [322] שו"ת מחז"א שם. [323]
פשוט. [324] שבות יצחק עמוד רנא בשם הגריש"א, מנח"י ח"ח
סימן יז, שבה"ל ח"ג סימן מז, וע"ע שש"כ סעיף פז בשם הגרשז"א
להתיר בכל אופן. [325] חוט שני עמוד קמנ, ופשוטו הוא לפי הנ"ל,
וע"ע זכור ושמור עמוד 69 והוא תמוה לכ'. [326] הלכות שבת
בשבת פ"ה סוף סעיף כב, שש"כ סעיף פו, ועיין ארחות שבת סוף
הערה קס שנוטה לאסור. [327] ספר ל"ט מלאכות עמוד 615 בשם
הגרמ"פ, שבה"ל ח"ט סימן נב, מכתב מהגרחפ"ש הובא בארצרות
השבת עמוד תקיט, וע"ע מנח"ש ח"ג סימן יב אות ט והובא ג"כ
בארחות שבת עמוד תקמב, ועיי"ש עמוד תקמ בשם הגריש"א.
[328] ארחות שבת עמוד תקמ בשם הגריש"א, הלכות שבת בשבת
פ"ה סעיף טז.

פרק יב - רחיצה בשבת (סימן שכו)

[329] שבת דף מ/א, סימן שכו, מ"ב סק"א. [330] שם. [331] ספר
הלכות שבת עמוד 387, זכור ושמור מבעיר עמוד 20, והוא ע"פ
אג"מ ח"ד סימן עד הלכות רחיצה אות א שכ' פחות ממדת החום
שדרך בני אדם לרחוץ בו, ועיין ארחות שבת ח"ב פכ"א הערה י
שכ' דלפי"ז מותר עד 38 מעלות, אבל עיי"ש בהערה ט שלפי
התהל"ד ושבה"ש מותר רק עד 37 מעלות וכן פסק במנח"י ח"ד
סימן מד אות כו. [332] ספר הלכות שבת עמוד 387 הערה
תתקלו בשם הגרמ"פ, זכור ושמור עמוד 20. [333] ערוה"ש סימן
שכו סעיף ב, ארחות שבת ח"ב פכ"א סעיף ה, שש"כ פי"ד סעיף ב.
[334] שש"כ סעיף ג, זכור ושמור עמוד 21. [335] זכור ושמור שם,
ארחות שבת סעיף ו. [336] ארחות שבת סעיף ח ע"פ שו"ע סימן
שלא סעיף ט. [337] ביה"ל ריש הס', ספר הלכות שבת עמוד 388,
שש"כ סעיף א. [338] סעיף ד, ה, ואע"ג דפליגי יש להחמיר כמ"ש
הגר"ז סעיף ד, וכ"כ ספר הלכות שבת עמוד 390, זכור ושמור עמוד

21. [339] שו"ת מהרי"ל החדשות סימן צו, תה"ד סימן רנה, מ"ב
סימן שכו ס"ק כא, שש"כ פי"ד סעיף יא. [340] שש"כ שם, ועיין
ארחות שבת פי"ג סעיף נא והערה פט. [341] מ"ב ס"ק ה, כה,
ועיין שש"כ פי"ד סק"א. [342] מ"ב סק"ז, שעה"צ סק"ה, שש"כ
הערה ד, ארחות שבת פכ"א הערה ל. [343] ערוה"ש סעיף י,
אג"מ ח"ד סימן עד אות ב, ארחות שבת סעיף טו, ספר הלכות שבת
עמוד 392. [344] ביה"ל סעיף ח ד"ה אדם, קצה"ש סימן קלג
סק"ח, אג"מ שם, ארחות שבת סעיף טז, יז.

פרק יג - הנאה ממעשה בישול בשבת

[345] סימן שיח סעיף א. [346] שם, מ"ב סק"ה. [347] ארחות
שבת ח"ג פכ"ה הערה כה בשם הרבה פוסקים. [348] מ"ב סק"ד.
[349] מ"ב סק"ז, ספר הלכות שבת עמוד 397. [350] ארחות שבת
ח"ג פכ"ה הערה טו, מאור השבת ח"א סימן יח הערה יז* בשם
הרבה פוסקים. [351] מ"ב סק"ו. [352] גר"ז סעיף ב. [353]
ביה"ל סימן שכה סעיף י ד"ה אינו יהודי. [354] סימן שיח סעיף א
ביה"ל ד"ה המבשל, חיי"א כלל ט סימן יא. [355] ארחות שבת
פכ"ה סעיף מא. [356] שם סעיף מב. [357] שם סעיף נד. [358]
סימן רנג סעיף א, מ"ב ס"ק מד, וסימן רנד סק"כ, חזו"א סימן לז ס"ק
כז ד"ה דינים העולים, ארחות שבת פכ"ה הערה ל, ועיין בספר
הלכות שבת עמוד 349 הערה תתקיא שיש להסתפק אם השיעור
כדי שיעשה היינו להתבשל כמאב"ד או כל צרכו. [359] מ"ב סימן
רנג סק"ה שם, חזו"א שם, ביה"ל ד"ה להשהותו עליה, הלכות שבת
בשבת פ"ה סעיף ל בדיני שהייה. [360] ביה"ל סימן רנג סעיף א
ד"ה ואם החזירו ישראל, חזו"א סימן לז ס"ק כז ד"ה היה צונן.
[361] מ"ב ס"ק לה, לו. ולעניין בני ביתו עיין פסק"ת הערה 104
שהחמיר ע"פ הגר"ז ומחה"ש, אבל עיין הלכות שבת בשבת
"חזרה" סעיף מ שהקיל ע"פ הב"ח, וכן משמע מסתימת המ"ב.
[362] ביה"ל סימן רנג סעיף ה ד"ה להחם בשם פרמ"ג, ארחות
שבת סעיף לט, הלכות שבת בשבת סעיף מ, וע"ע חזו"א סימן לז
ס"ק כז ד"ה ומבואר. ויש לעיין למה אוכל קר אינו יכול להיות
מצטמק ויפה לו. [363] ספר הלכות שבת עמוד 367 הערה תתשג.
[364] מ"ב סימן רנז סק"ח. [365] עיקר הדין בסימן רנז סעיף א,
ולעניין מאכל ב"ד עיין ביה"ל ד"ה י"א וחזו"א סימן לז ס"ק כה ד"ה
ומידו, ולעניין המתנה בכדי שיעשה עיין קצה"ש סימן עא ס"ק כח,
ולעניין המתנה עד שיתקרר עיין ביה"ל סימן רנג סעיף ה ד"ה להחם
בשם פרמ"ג, ולעניין חימום מחדש באופן המותר עיין ארחות שבת
פ"ב סעיף קו, ולעניין הטמין לצורך היום עיין רמ"א על עיקר הדין.
[366] שם. [367] מ"ב סימן רנז סק"י. [368] מ"ב סימן שיח סק"ב.
[369] לעניין מאכל ב"ד עיין מ"ב סימן שיח ס"ק כז. לעניין בישול
אחר אפייה עיין מ"ב שם ס"ק מו. לעניין בישול אחר בישול בדבר

לח עיין ארחות שבת פכ"ה הערה עו. לענין מצקת עיין מ"ב ס"ק מה. לענין דבר גוש עיין מ"ב ס"ק קיח. [370] מבית לוי ח"ו עמוד לג אות ח, עיין מקורות 271. [371] עיין מקורות שם. [372] עיין מקורות שם. [373] סימן שיח סעיף ב, מ"ב ס"ק יא.

May the learning of
this **ספר** be **לעילוי נשמת**
and a **זכות** for the **נשמות**
of our dear parents

ר׳ יצחק ב״ר גדליה ז״ל
מרת אסתר בת ר׳ פישל הכהן ע״ה
ר׳ אליעזר ב״ר ראובן הלוי ז״ל
מרת שפרה רבקה בת ר׳ מאיר יוסף
ע״ה

Dedicated by
Judith and Ira Weiss

ת.נ.צ.ב.ה.

לע"נ

ר' יוסף שמואל ב"ר אלעזר ז"ל

מרת חנה רחל בת ר' יצחק אריה הכהן ע"ה

Dedicated in Memory
Of our Beloved Parents

Samuel Joseph and Anne Rachela
Barclay

ת.נ.צ.ב.ה.

לע"נ

ר' ישראל ב"ר מאיר טרעפ ז"ל
ואשתו מרת פיגא הענניא
בת ר' עובדי' הלוי ע"ה

ת.נ.צ.ב.ה.

May the learning of this ספר be a זכות
לעילוי נשמות and be
For our beloved parents

ר׳ שלמה ב״ר זכריה ז״ל

מרת מינה בת ר׳ דוד ברוך ע״ה

Henry and Chaya Bauer
Cecil and Lilian Wolpe

ת.נ.צ.ב.ה.

May the learning of this ספר be a זכות and be
לעילוי נשמות
For our beloved parents

ר׳ זאב ב״ר משה נח ז״ל
מרת גליקה בת ר׳ שלמה זלמן ע״ה
ר׳ שרגא פייוול ב״ר מנחם מנדל ז״ל

ת.נ.צ.ב.ה.

ולזכות מרת בריינדל צביה בת ר׳ אריה לייב תחי׳
לאריכות ימים ושנים

Dedicated by the Vanning and the Berkman Families

לע״נ

ר׳ הירש בן ציון בן ר׳ זלמן מרדכי הכהן ז״ל

מרת לאה בת ר׳ אברהם ע״ה

ת.נ.צ.ב.ה.

May the learning of this ספר be a זכות
for our beloved parents

ר׳ שלמה ב״ר יעקב יוסף הלוי ז״ל

מרת חיה בת ר׳ פסח ע״ה

ר׳ שמואל שניאור ב״ר יצחק יעקב ז״ל

מרת מרים בת ר׳ שרגא ע״ה

Along with our sister

מרת חיה חנה בת ר׳ שמואל שניאור ע״ה

Dedicated by the Sherwood family

ת.נ.צ.ב.ה.

Dedicated
in the memory of
my grandparents

Mr Iscka & Mrs Rosie Emanuel

formerly of Manchester
and Yerushalayim

תנצב״ה

May the learning of this ספר
be a זכות and עילוי נשמה
for our beloved parents

ר' גדליה ב"ר יצחק יוסף ז"ל

מרת לאה מלכה בת ר' פסח ע"ה

ת.נ.צ.ב.ה.